UPHOLSTERY
PROPERLY
EXPLAIN

Paperfronts are the world's leading series of low-price practical books. The series covers a wide range of "How to . . ." subjects ranging from cookery and pets to motoring and sports and pastimes. Always ask for *Paperfronts* when you need practical information.

UPHOLSTERY PROPERLY EXPLAINED

by

Anne Brock

PAPERFRONTS
ELLIOT RIGHT WAY BOOKS
KINGSWOOD, SURREY, U.K.

Made and Printed in Great Britain by
Love & Malcomson Ltd., Redhill, Surrey.

CONTENTS

INTRODUCTION

"Are you sitting comfortably? If not why not!" Perhaps because you have never thought of upholstering your own chair before, is that why not?

Maybe you don't really know one end of a hammer from the other and would feel a little bit scared at the prospect. After all, what would you find inside the chair, and for that matter where and just how does one start? This book is written for you.

It is not difficult to upholster a simple chair, with care. Be brave, take the plunge and let this book be your guide step by step through one of the examples described in the following pages. But do start with something simple – learn to walk before you run, after all in bygone days an upholsterer had to serve a seven year apprenticeship.

Being realistic, those who sit in an office generally find upholstery a pleasant change; those who don't know one end of a needle from the other soon find out which is the pointed end of a tack. Those who, on occasion, have been known to be near losing control of their tempers soon discover the therapeutic value of upholstering a chair and banging in tacks rather than banging doors!

This book is intended to be something of a beginner's dictionary in that the four basic ways of traditional upholstery will be found in the examples chosen, i.e. the simplest of all a pincushion seat, the seat of the Ottoman or stool, the overstuffed, or unsprung seat, and finally the sprung seat. More complicated chairs, sofas, etc., upholstered in the traditional method, are all adaptations of these examples.

The same applies to the examples quoted for foam upholstery. The pincushion seat is an example of a rounded edge to a seat and the dining room chair seat an example of a straight-sided seat.

Which method do you choose, the modern method using foam or the traditional method using hair and hessian? Generally my advice is to use the same as what comes off the chair. The man who designed your chair, designed it with a particular method and material in mind, therefore unless there is a good reason for change – use the same again.

However some chairs look quite as well whichever way they are upholstered, so if you are feeling at all diffident, go for foam.

However one word of caution : you will see that foam has many advantages, but it does also have one disadvantage and that is fire – fire and foam just do not mix. Being a by-product of petrol, once alight, foam burns easily and has very toxic fumes. So beware when having a cigarette in your chair! However, research is going on all the time to find ways of overcoming this problem.

Having tackled your first chair satisfactorily, you will have given your morale a boost, gained an insight into up-holstery and have come to the conclusion that upholstery either definitely is, or is not, for you. If the former, you will be itching to try something more ambitious; if the latter, well, at least you will now be sitting comfortably!

Start your upholstery at a time when you have a relatively free week or weekend ahead of you; it is going to take you several hours work and you will begin to understand why a professional upholsterer charges so much to reupholster your chair.

Before starting to strip your chair, read the sections on "introducing your tools" and "materials", then turn to the shopping list at the appropriate chapter; measure and buy the materials needed.

Be sure too that you have your tools handy. There is nothing more annoying than to discover after your shopping expedition that your hammer has a broken handle and the only scissors in the house are a pair of nail scissors.

The sitting room is not the best place for stripping furniture. You will find a tremendous amount of dust and dirt comes out of your chair, however house-proud you think you are. A garden shed or the garden on a fine day is ideal or an uncarpeted room your second choice. If you decide to strip your chair in the garage beware not to leave a single tack on the floor; the car tyres will be sure to find it if you do.

Supplies of upholstery materials are not always easy to find. Even do-it-yourself shops do not keep all the materials you are likely to need. Your best bet is to look under "upholsterers" in the yellow pages of your telephone book, preferably choosing one with a High Street shop, explain your requirements in the nicest possible way and ask for his help in supplying you.

This Book has come to be written after many years of repeated requests from my students to write a book in simple English with some line drawings to help them refresh their memories when I am not around to remind them of what they were told in their classes, and for those studying for City & Guilds part 1 Upholstery, here is all you need to know.

So to them and to all my readers may I wish you the very best of luck and comfortable sitting in the future.

Introducing Tools

Most of the tools used in upholstery can be found about the house already. If you can't find them or haven't got them, it will not be a waste of money to buy them. They are all useful tools.

Mallet and an old *chisel* or *screwdriver* for taking out tacks. If you have no mallet use the long flat side of the hammer head. However it is kinder to the wooden handle of a tool to use a wooden mallet.

Pincers: Useful for removing tacks with broken heads.

Small-headed hammer: Since the tacks are small, use a

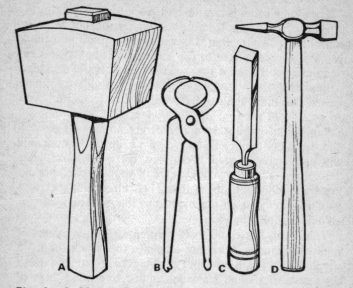

Fig. 1 *A*: Mallet, *B*: Pincers, *C*: Chisel (only use an *old* chisel for taking out tacks as it will be no good for woodwork afterwards), *D*: Hammer.

small-headed hammer (not a "claw" hammer). A special upholsterer's cabriole hammer is not necessary and indeed a hammer with a magnetic head can be dangerous. It is very easy to put a tack into your finger instead of into the chair when the tack is held by the hammer magnetically.

Web stretcher: A special web stretcher can be expensive. A piece of good strong wood approximately 50mm (2″) wide by 150mm (6″) long will serve the purpose quite as well.

Scissors: A good pair of scissors, that are sharp and cut right to their points are essential.

Tape measure.

Needles: An 8″ or 10″ upholsterer's needle (i.e. a double-ended needle) and a packet of mixed half-circular needles.

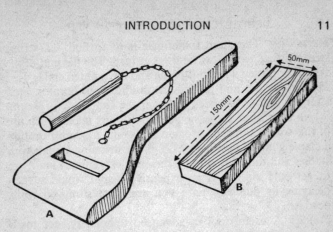

Fig. 2. Web stretcher, *A*: The purchased article, *B*: A block of wood will do just as well.

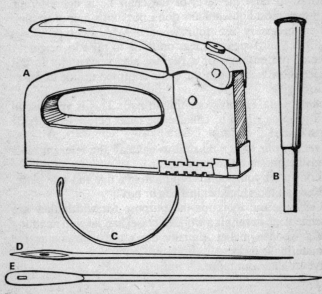

Fig. 3. *A*: Staple gun, *B*: Punch, *C*: Half-circular needle, *D*: Upholsterer's needle, *E*: Regulator.

Regulator: These are sometimes hard to find – a strong steel knitting needle can be used instead. The flat end of the regulator is used when buttoning and the pointed end is used for evening out and poking the stuffing into corners, etc., after the canvas has been put over the stuffing.

Staple gun: Most professional upholsterers make much use of this today. For the Ottoman and some modern furniture a staple gun is a positive blessing, but stripping a chair with staples is a different matter; they are exceedingly stubborn to get out! As this is an expensive item I would suggest delaying its purchase until you are quite sure you really need it.

Punch: A useful tool in advanced upholstery, not really necessary for use with a simple chair.

Trestles: A professional upholsterer will use a pair of trestles, to raise the level of the chair he is upholstering. However most householders don't boast of a pair of trestles. When necessary use four wooden Windsor type chairs and put your four chair legs on these to raise its height. A pair of old cushions or a rug are also very useful to put under show wood when the chair is turned upside down or onto its side.

Thumb nail: Finally your thumb nail. This is very useful as a prop on which to balance the tacks before hammering them home!

Note, re your tools: Be sure to have all the relevant tools ready before starting on your chair.

Look after your tools, keep them in a dry and safe place. Keep all tools together in a bag or box.

Only use the tools for the purpose for which they are intended, i.e. never hit a wooden chisel handle with anything but a wooden mallet. Equally don't use your mallet for hammering in tacks.

Never lend your tools.

Introducing the Materials Used in Upholstery

At the start of each chapter there is a shopping list; consult this list, together with your chair, for the exact amount of materials needed.

Tacks: The nails used in upholstery are called "tacks". When buying the tacks be sure to buy "cut tacks" and not "bayonet tacks" as supplied by most hardware and do-it-yourself stores. Upholstery tacks have large heads and very sharp pointed ends.

When cut tacks are labelled as "improved" they have larger heads and fatter bodies than the "fine" tacks. "Blued" tacks have sharper points still.

The tack should be small enough so as not to split the wood and large enough to hold the materials in place. As a general rule buy : –

16mm ($\frac{5}{8}''$) improved tacks for webbing and laid cord.
13mm ($\frac{1}{2}''$) fine for hessian, scrim and top cover.
10mm ($\frac{3}{8}''$) fine for top cover on delicate chair frames.

Webbing: There are three sorts of webbing in general use : –
Pirelli which is elasticated and is used to take the place of springs under foam upholstery;
Black and white webbing is the best and longest lasting for traditional upholstery. This comes in various widths, 2" (50mm) being the most usual;
Jute webbing, generally beige in colour, it is not as strong as the black and white and should only be used for chair backs.
Springs: This book is only concerned with coil springs, although serpentine, zig-zag, spring units, etc. are all in use in chairs today. The size as well as the gauge should be considered and for a small chair seat a 5" spring of 10 gauge would be adequate.
Hessian:
Tarpaulin or spring hessian is for covering springs or webbing where the greatest strength is required. It can be bought in widths of 36" or 72".
Scrim is an open weave type of hessian used for covering the

first stuffing of hair or fibre which is then stitched into shape. Better quality scrim is made from flax.

10oz hessian can be used for covering the webbing on a small chair where the strength of spring hessian may not be needed. It can also be used instead of scrim to cover the first stuffing. It can be bought in widths of 36" or 72".

Stuffing/Filling: The main stuffings used are:–

Horse hair, which is undoubtedly the finest filling. The best quality comes from the tails and manes of horses. A poorer quality comes from cattle and pigs. Often it is dyed black. The longer and curlier, the better the quality.

Cheaper than hair is **Black Fibre** made from Algerian grass. Usually dyed black but sometimes left green. The black keeps its curl better.

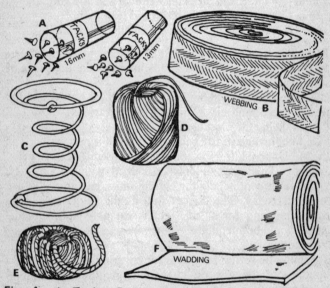

Fig. 4. *A*: Tacks, *B*: Webbing, *C*: A spring, *D*: Twine, *E*: Laid cord, *F*: Wadding.

Coconut fibre or curly coir comes from the outside of the coconut. The longer the fibre the better the quality but it is not as easy or as nice to work with as black fibre.

You may find your chair has been stuffed with a variety of other fillings such as wood shavings, wool, seaweed, etc., plus an odd dead beetle or two!

Laid cord: A strong twine or cord for lashing the tops of the springs into position.

Twine: Upholsterer's twine is very strong, easy to use and doesn't end up in knots – or with care it doesn't! It is used for stitching the stuffing into position. It is expensive but worth buying. Kitchen or garden string just isn't strong enough and it is false economy to buy it.

Wadding: Wadding can be made from natural fibres such as cotton or wool, or from synthetics. It comes in various qualities and thicknesses and is used to prevent the hair or fibres working their way through to the top of the seat.

Calico: Unbleached calico, bought in various qualities and widths is used as a final covering before the top cover is put on. Although not essential, its use is recommended, for amongst other reasons it is a trial run before putting on the final cover.

Adhesives: Use a clear adhesive for attaching the gimp or braid. This is generally sold in tubes. Use an adhesive recommended for use with foam when sticking the calico strips to the foam.

Gimp pins: Very small pins. Buy gimp pins in a colour to match the braid. When in use their heads blend in well with the background and don't show. Also used to secure the top cover where there is to be no braid and normal tacks would look ugly. Gimp pins should be used in conjunction with an adhesive, putting one at corners and every 200-250mm (8"-10") in between to help secure the braid in the years to come.

Black cloth: A cheap black fabric used to cover the underside of the seat after it has been re-upholstered.

Introducing Foam

With the introduction of foam cushioning some fifty years ago, there is no excuse for anyone not to be sitting comfortably. Foam has made things so much easier for the first-time upholsterer.

If you are not sitting comfortably and the idea of re-upholstering your chair slightly scares you, start your upholstering by using foam. It is a little more expensive than using traditional materials but you can't go wrong using foam.

What is foam? Foam used for upholstery is made either from natural latex or from synthetics.

Latex is the liquid from the trees called *Havea Brasiliensis*, which only grow in certain countries and within a few hundred miles either side of the equator. Because each tree oozes only a small amount of the liquid every other day, the cost of collecting the latex, transporting and manufacturing it into foam, all make the final cost of a latex foam cushion rather expensive.

Synthetic foam is made from *Polyurethane*, a by-product of the petro-chemical industry and called *Polyether*.

Both latex and polyether foam are moulded into various cushion shapes or in sheet form and are also made in various densities depending upon the amount of air mixed in during the foam's manufacture.

Choose foam of a density suitable for the job in question, i.e. foam for chair backs and arms should be 14-23 kgs and 27-51 kgs for seats.

Both latex and synthetics are moulded into and termed "pincore", "cavity" and "plain". Pincore has a mass of small holes going right through the foam from top to bottom. Cover pincore foam with a layer of synthetic wadding before putting on the top cover, to ensure the holes don't show through.

Cavity has a series of larger holes. The top of the foam is smooth all over and the underside shows the large 50mm (2″) square holes. Cavity foam is generally used in car seating.

Plain foam is what most shops sell. It can be bought in thicknesses from 13mm ($\frac{1}{2}''$) up to 100mm ($4''$) or more. Generally it is to be found in large sheets which the shop keeper has either cut into smaller pieces or will cut to the required size for you.

Foam, for a beginner, has the advantage over traditional upholstery in that there are no springs to be lashed nor edges to be sewn into shape. It is also a lot cleaner and tidier.

Pirelli webbing under foam takes the place of the webbing and the springs, and the end result will be quite as comfortable, if not more so.

If putting foam on top of ordinary webbing instead of Pirelli webbing, tack a piece of calico or hessian to the chair frame between the webbing and the foam to prevent the webbing cutting into the foam.

If putting foam on a solid base, drill air holes in the base so as to allow the foam to breathe.

Always cover your foam with a calico cover before putting on the top cover fabric. Strong sunlight can cause damage to foams, especially to latex foam, and a calico cover will go a long way to preventing this. It also makes a trial run before putting on your top cover and will certainly recoup its cost by adding considerably to the life of the top fabric.

If your chair is already upholstered with foam, remove the top cover fabric, look carefully at the foam and smell it. If there is a suspicion of a smell, however faint, if the foam looks brittle or if you have any doubts as to the probable length of life left in the foam, discard it. It would be a pity for the foam to crumble before the top fabric has worn out.

Before buying your foam it is worth making a template in thick paper or cardboard of the parts of your chair that need to be covered in foam. Sometimes the shopkeeper will cut the pieces of foam to the exact size and shape you require. When measuring for foam, add 13mm ($\frac{1}{2}''$) onto all measurements.

Cutting your own foam is not difficult provided you remember:

Mark round the edges of the template with a marking pen or a thick ended biro on to the foam.

Cut the foam if over 25mm (1″) with a long bladed serrated knife or razor blade.

Make a long shallow downward cut in the foam drawing the knife along the top of the marked line using a steel straight edge if possible.

Hold the knife at a 45° angle and make several shallow cuts to get to the end of the line rather than trying to cut through the complete thickness of the foam in one movement. This is because the foam tries to move with the knife.

Scissors can be used when cutting foam of 25mm (1″) or less thick. However it is difficult to get a straight vertical edge as the foam will bulge as it is cut.

Cutting foam for a cushion: Cut the foam 10mm ($\frac{1}{2}$″) bigger than the size you actually require, thus the foam fits snugly into the sides and corners of the cushion cover and pushes out any wrinkles.

When cutting foam into a rounded or curved shape, sandwich the foam between two pieces of cardboard or hardboard templates, securing them with a piece of wire or strong twine threaded through their middles. By cutting round both templates in this way you will get good straight edges.

For a rounded effect on the edges of the loose cushion, put adhesive on the sides, allow to became tacky and pinch together, so the edge of the top meets the edge of the bottom.

All foam intended to stay permanently on the chair should have strips of calico stuck to the side of the pieces of foam and then tacked with 13mm tacks to the chair frame.

Leave adhesive long enough to dry hard, i.e. overnight. After the adhesive is dry, dust along all joints between the calico and the foam with talcum powder to stop stickiness, before tacking to the chair frame.

Foam can be built up to the thickness required, i.e. two pieces of 50mm (2″) thick foam stuck together will make a

100mm (4″) thick cushion. The seat can be domed (i.e. rounded top) by putting a piece of 25mm (1″) thick foam between the two larger pieces. Cut this smaller piece of foam 75mm (3″) smaller than the chair seat. Feather the edges by cutting away a triangle along each edge at a 45° angle.

Considerations Before Buying Top Cover Fabric

Serious consideration must be given to the quality, design and colour when choosing the fabric for the top cover. Because of the cost involved the fabric will have to remain serviceable and please the eye of the beholder for several years.

Remember some colours are restful, some warm, others cold and some can positively cause irritation and annoyance. Hard, bright and clashing colours are the chief offenders.

Always buy the best you can afford, not necessarily the most expensive, but that which is of good value.

Buy firm, closely woven fabric and check that it has been specially woven for upholstery purposes. A loosely woven fabric will not wear as well and will attract the dirt.

A dark coloured fabric as opposed to a pale coloured fabric will show grubby marks less obviously. The same applies to a patterned fabric.

Consider pattern repeat and where the pattern falls in relation to the width, is there likely to be much wastage?

Remember that the pattern must be centered and might therefore require more yardage than a plain fabric.

Check the pattern is on the straight of grain.

Inspect for flaws. These should be marked with a coloured tag, but may not be.

Never buy curtaining or dress fabrics, they are not strong enough to wear well.

Buy sufficient fabric to complete your chair or chairs. You may not be able to repeat later.

Ask to see the fabric in a natural light; artificial light alters colours.

Remember that the fabric must run from the bottom to the top of the chair back and arms, and from front to back of the chair seats.

Buy your fabric as wide as possible. This is usually more economical in the long run.

Look for the maker's name. If no name, the maker can't be too proud of his fabric.

It is often easier for the beginner to leave the buying of the top cover fabric until after the chair has been upholstered and the calico cover is on. You will have a better picture in your mind's eye at that stage.

If your chair is a period piece, the new top cover fabric should be period in design also.

Bear in mind not only the style of the chair and the colour of the show wood, but also the style and colourings of the room in which the chair will be used.

Do take your shopping list and measurements with you on your shopping expedition, also samples of colours that need to be matched, i.e. the carpet, curtains or other chairs in the room.

Among suitable upholstery fabrics are: brocade, brocatelle, corduroy, damask, denim, tapestry, repp, velvet including Dralon, P.V.C. coated fabrics and leather. However, leather is not for beginners – look at the price and you will know why!

Braids and gimp

These can be bought by the metre or yard. They should be as near a match as possible to the colour of the top cover fabric and be sufficiently wide to cover the heads of the tacks.

Stripping and Preparing the Chair Frame

Put on old clothes; stripping is often a dirty job!

Old tacks should be removed with an old ripping chisel,

tack remover, or 10mm ($\frac{3}{8}''$) wide screwdriver, and a mallet, working in the direction of the grain of the wood. If you work against the grain, there is a danger of splitting the wood.

Place the sharp end of the screwdriver or chisel up against or underneath the head of the tack if possible, following the grain of wood, give the screwdriver, tack remover or chisel a sharp tap or two with the mallet and, hopefully, out will pop the tack, head and all.

If the head comes off the tack or if it is a bit stubborn to come out, use a pair of pincers. If you don't have a pair of pincers, the claw end of a hammer can be used, but be careful not to damage the show wood with the head of the hammer by careless use.

It is advisable to approach the work of stripping in a systematic way. Generally, stripping should be carried out in the reverse order to that in which the chair was originally upholstered. Start by turning your chair upside down and remove the bottom canvas from your chair. You can then see the extent of the re-upholstery needed.

If the webbing is broken, frayed or badly sagging – re-upholster.

If the webbing is sagging slightly, but the rest of the seat is in good order, tighten webbing by taking out the tacks at one end of a strip of webbing, tighten webbing with a hide stretcher, grippers, pinchers or similar.

Or add new strips of webbing in each direction over the top of the existing webbing, but this is poor workmanship really!

Perhaps you will only need to put a new top cover on. In this case remove the tacks from the old top cover fabric only, add a layer of cotton or the thinner terylene wadding if necessary and recover.

However, having taken off the top cover, then the calico and wadding, you may find the hessian holding the stuffing has worn. It is then advisable either to cover the existing hessian with another piece of hessian, tacking it to the bevelled edge of the top of the chair seat with 13mm tacks and sewing round the top of the seat edge (again bad practice), or to completely strip your chair.

If you are in fact stripping a sofa, chaise longue or a chair with a padded back and arms, only strip the seat of the upholstery. In most cases the basic upholstery of the back and arms will far outlive that of the seat which comes in for a hard life.

Having turned your chair upside down and removed the black cloth or similar, remove every visible tack from the bottom and sides of the chair's bottom rail.

Depending on the type of chair it may be that the outside back's top cover fabric comes down to the bottom of the chair, in which case remove it completely taking out all tacks and cutting the stitching. It may also be necessary to remove completely the outside arm's top cover fabric in order to remove the seat.

Then make sure to remove every tack that it is possible to remove from the wood where you are working. It is easier to do it while stripping than to find a new tack being bent while it is driven into an old tack at a later date.

Once you have taken out all visible tacks, with a little bit of luck and ingenuity the seat will come away from the chair frame. Obviously some chairs are a lot easier than others in that you can see where the tacks are. With a sofa or an upholstered arm chair you can't always.

Leave the top cover fabric on the inside arms and inside back of the chair or sofa while you recover the seat as far as the calico stage. Then remove the inside arm and inside back covers, add a layer of wadding and recover with the new top cover fabric.

It will probably take you a couple of hours to strip your chair seat, but take heart. This preliminary job is by far the worst and most back-aching job of all. Once completed the fun part will follow.

Having stripped your chair, feed the wood with your own home-made furniture reviver (see recipe on page 25).

If your chair has springs, test each spring after removing it from the chair by placing the spring on a table or the floor, place the palm of your hand across the top coil of the spring and depress it. If the spring is resistant to pressure and goes down straight, as opposed to crookedly. then it may be used again. If in any doubt, discard the spring.

Save and wash any horse hair found in the chair; to wash it, see page 26.

Always remove and discard the old top cover whether or not you are going to re-upholster your chair completely. Old top covers will have become worn and dirty over the years and will mark the new top cover fabric if left on underneath.

Woodworm

Inspect for woodworm. Signs of active worm are a powdery dust and light-coloured holes in the wood itself. Worm holes that are no longer active or that have been treated will be dark in colour.

Treat active worm with a proprietary brand of woodworm killer. A very effective way is to inject one hole in every square inch with woodworm fluid, and then paint or spray the fluid over all parts of the chair, particularly underneath and in dark corners.

Woodworms like soft wood in preference to hard wood, and natural wood to polished wood, so the underside of the seat frame is a favourite haunt. Once your chair has become home to a pair of woodworms, they soon multiply and travel to other pieces of furniture in the room. So treat as soon as worm is suspected and keep an eye on it afterwards for a while. Woodworm holes can be filled with a mixture of sawdust and glue. Sandpaper smooth when dry.

A word of warning here, most woodworm killer fluids, by their nature are very penetrating, and the top cover fabric should not be attached to your chair too soon after application.

Structural Defects

If your chair is not structurally sound, then it is not worth re-upholstering. A common fault with dining room type chairs is that their legs become weak at their joints – caused by those people who tilt their chairs backwards while sitting on them and balancing on the two back legs! The chair should be taken apart, the dowels, mortice and tenons cleaned and re-glued. Corner blocks can be fitted into the corners, glued and screwed in for extra strength.

Use a proprietary brand of wood glue and be sure to follow the directions on the container carefully and use as recommended. If you are not happy about doing the repairs yourself, take your chair to an established carpenter.

Polish and Varnish

Do not strip the patina from your chair, a finish which has taken years of loving care, polish and elbow grease to build up. Once the patina has been removed only time and care can replace.

If your chair has been stained or varnished, this is a different matter. At the top of the inside of a front leg rub a patch with the edge of a coin or with your thumb nail, and if the leg has been varnished at some time there will be a scratch mark.

Varnish can be removed by gently rubbing the wood with No. 000 wire wool and methylated spirits. This will soften the old varnish which needs to be wiped off with plenty of old rags or kitchen roll paper. Use an old toothbrush and methylated spirits to get into difficult corners or some cotton wool on the end of an orange stick.

It is advisable to wear rubber gloves and put plenty of newspaper underneath the chair before you start stripping. Paint stripper is not recommended, because it raises the grain and makes it difficult to get a good polish on the wood afterwards.

Having stripped off the old varnish either apply two coats

of furniture reviver with a twenty-four hour interval between coats or apply a coat of clear polyseal, an oil based stain, or leave the wood natural and use a good quality wax polish or make your own from beeswax and turpentine (see below for recipe).

Do not cut the new top cover using the old as a pattern; the new one seldom fits when cut this way. Old top covers can be used as a rough guide only when estimating for the fabric needed for the new top cover. Be generous and allow plenty extra in case the new seat is built up higher.

Recipe for Furniture Reviver

4 fluid oz. raw linseed oil.
4 fluid oz. malt vinegar.
2 teaspoonfuls methylated spirits.

METHOD: Put the linseed oil in a ½ pint sized bottle, add the methylated spirits and shake well to mix.

Add the vinegar a little at a time and shake well again before adding more.

Shake the bottle well before use as the mixture will separate.

Apply with a clean rag or brush to your chair frame after stripping, to feed the wood.

Recipe for Furniture Polish

3 oz. beeswax.
½ pint white spirit.

METHOD: Grate the beeswax and put with the white spirits into an old clean coffee jar or similar in a warm place, such as on top of a warm radiator. Shake from time to time. The two ingredients will blend together and produce a good polish.

Apply to your polished furniture by using one part of

polish to ninety-nine parts of elbow grease – i.e. plenty of rubbing and not too much polish!

Washing Horse Hair

Half fill a sink or basin with tepid water. Do not add any soap powder or detergent.

Undo the old stitching and discard as much of the old hessian or scrim cover as possible from the old chair seat of horse hair. Pull the hair roughly apart in small handfuls and immerse in the water, discarding all pieces of twine, tacks and other rubbish.

Rinse in a clean lot of water.

Put the wet hair in an old pillowcase and spin in a spin drier.

Spread the hair out on a sheet or on a newspaper in a warm room or in the sun to dry completely before using.

Upholsterer's Knots

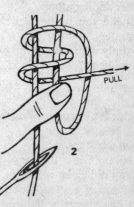

Fig. 5. Upholsterer's knot.

If you find a proper upholsterer's knot a bit difficult to master, here is a very good second best knot which you may find easier.

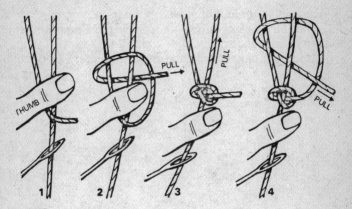

Fig. 6. Upholsterer's knot – second best.

1

DROP-IN PINCUSHION SEAT
(TRADITIONAL UPHOLSTERY)

SHOPPING LIST

. . . m/yds webbing	. . . m/yds top cover fabric
. . . m/yds hessian	. . . m/yds braid
. . . lbs stuffing	16mm ($\frac{5}{8}$″) tacks
. . . m/yds wadding (cotton)	13mm ($\frac{1}{2}$″) tacks
. . . m/yds calico	Gimp pins
Twine	Black cloth (optional)
Adhesive for braid	

You can take the measurements for your shopping list before actually stripping your chair seat. However if you have a drop-in seat, take this out of the frame to measure.

Turn your chair or frame upside down. If there is a piece of black cloth or similar fabric tacked to the bottom of your frame covering the webbing, remove this fabric so you can see the webbing. There is no need to remove any more of the upholstery materials before measuring. Measure over the top of the old cover for the moment and strip later.

If you have a chair with a pincushion seat and no drop-in frame, this will be worked in the same way and you must measure in the same way but miss out the calico stage. This is because the rebate of the chair is usually so narrow that it cannot take too many tacks.

WEBBING: Measure that part of each length of webbing that you can actually see, and add 100mm (4″) to each length, i.e. 25mm (1″) at each end hidden from view and 25mm (1″) for turnunders.

50mm (2″) wide black and white webbing is the ideal to use.

Add together the measurements of the strands of webbing making sure that the gap between each strand of webbing is no more than 50mm (2″). (If you buy webbing 38mm (1½″) wide, the space between each strand should be 38mm (1½″).)

Round this figure up by 250mm-300mm (10″-12″) so as to have some webbing over. You will need this to be able to stretch the webbing tightly round the web stretcher on the final strand.

HESSIAN (either 10oz or 12oz): Measure the width across the underside of the frame and add 50mm (2″). Do likewise with the length.

STUFFING: If there is horse hair in your seat, and you will see little hairs poking through the old hessian, wash it and re-use it. Otherwise buy 1 lb of hair, black fibre or curly coir for a small size chair seat.

COTTON WADDING: Measure over the top of the seat from the edge of one side of the frame across to the edge of the other side. No need to add anything to the width measurement here. Do likewise with the length.

CALICO: Measure as for the wadding but add 50mm (2″) to the length and 50mm (2″) to the width measurements. Omit the calico if you are working straight onto the chair frame.

TACKS: 2oz of 16mm and 4oz of 13mm upholsterer's tacks, not bayonet tacks. However if the wood on the top of your frame is only 25mm (1") or so wide, it would be safer and less likely to split the wood if you were to use 13mm ($\frac{1}{2}$") tacks instead of the 16mm ($\frac{5}{8}$") tacks for the webbing. Likewise drop down one size and use 10mm ($\frac{3}{8}$") instead of 13mm ($\frac{1}{2}$") tacks for the hessian and calico, etc.

TWINE: If you can't persuade an upholsterer or supplier to sell you a small hank of approximately twenty yards or so of upholsterer's twine, then use a really strong string which doesn't break easily.

TOP COVER: The measurements for the top cover will be the same as those for the calico.

BRAID OR GIMP: For a drop-in seat you will not need braid because all the tacks will be hidden from view. However if you are tacking straight onto the chair frame, measure round the edge of the showwood and add 25mm (1") for turnings. This is the amount of braid you will need to buy.

Having done your shopping and bought the necessary materials, gather up the tools needed for the next job which is to strip your chair or stool seat. Please turn back to the introduction (see page 20). Don't forget to give the wood some attention before re-upholstering (see page 25).

The word "drop-in" means that your seat has been made up on a frame and dropped into the chair frame or stool frame when completed. "Pincushion" is the name given to the type of seat, i.e. like a pincushion with no sewn sides.

It may be that your pincushion chair has no drop-in seat frame. If this is the case, work in the same way as described but attach all materials to the rebate on the inside of the chair. A word of caution here, if the rebate on your chair is narrow and delicate, you should use 13mm improved tacks to hold the webbing instead of 16mm improved tacks, so as to avoid the danger of splitting the wood. The narrow rebate may well split if five tacks are used, therefore use four tacks in the following formation:

o   o

   o   o

If your drop-in seat frame is a rather tight fit in your chair or stool, it may be necessary to shave a little of the wood off from the sides of the frame, bearing in mind that both the calico and your top cover fabric will have to go between the seat frame and the chair frame.

WEBBING

Use 50mm (2″) wide black and white webbing. 16mm (⅝″) improved tacks should be used for attaching the webbing to the seat.

If your seat frame has a bevelled edge on one side of the frame, this is the top and this is the side on which you will put the webbing.

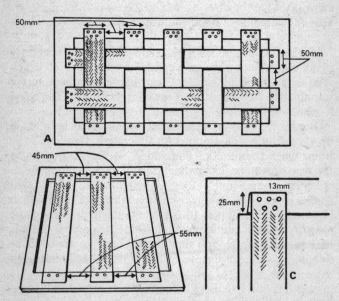

Fig. 7. *A*: How to space the webbing on an oblong stool,
B: Chair seat frame where the front is wider than the back,
C: Attaching the first piece of webbing.

The strands of webbing should be evenly spaced and the space between each piece of webbing should never be wider than the width of the webbing (see fig. 7A). The new webbing should be placed slightly to one side of where the old webbing was attached to avoid using the same tack holes. On small drop-in chair seats there should be at least two strands of webbing in each direction or three strands in each direction on larger drop-in chair seats.

If your seat is oblong, such as a stool, you will need more strands of webbing on the longer side than on the shorter side (see fig. 7A).

If the front of the frame is wider than the back, place one piece of webbing down the centre from the back of the frame to the front. Then place another strand of webbing on either side evenly spaced between the web in the centre and the inside edge of the frame, so that it slightly splays outwards at the front rail (see fig. 7B).

Take your piece of webbing, turn under 25mm (1″) and place it 13mm (½″) in from the edge of the seat rail (see fig. 7C). Secure with five 16mm (⅝″) tacks in the formation as shown. Do not cut the webbing yet.

All tacks must be driven straight down into the wood. A tack head that is badly hammered in and not flush with the wood will damage the webbing.

If the top of your seat frame is an inch or so wide only, it will be too narrow to put five tacks in as described above without splitting the wood, therefore hammer in four tacks in the formation shown in fig. 8A.

Remember that the webbing will stretch slightly over the years, therefore you must attach the webbing to the other side of the frame under tension and as tautly as possible.

Either use a web stretcher or take a piece of wood approximately 50mm (2″) wide, wind the webbing over the top of the wood, back underneath and up to cover the end nearest the seat rail.

Tighten the webbing sufficiently round the wood so the wood is just held upwards at a 45° angle by the webbing

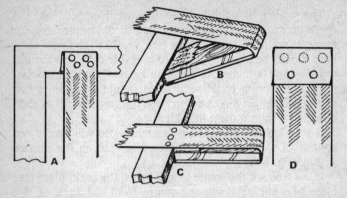

Fig. 8. *A*: Tack formation if the seat frame is narrow, *B*: Tensioning with a piece of wood, *C*: Tacking after tensioning, *D*: The final two tacks.

(see fig. 8B). Tension the webbing by pressing downwards on the wood until it is at the horizontal with the seat rail, the webbing should now be very taut. Put in three 16mm ($\frac{5}{8}''$) tacks in a straight line, one third of the way in from the outside edge of the seat rail, being one tack in each corner and one tack in the centre of the webbing (see fig. 8C).

Turn the piece of webbing back on itself and hammer in two more tacks in a line nearer to the centre of the seat than the other three tacks and in between them (see fig. 8D).

Cut the webbing 13mm ($\frac{1}{2}''$) away from the tacks. Complete all the webbing in one direction first before starting to web in the other direction.

When webbing in the other direction, the webbing must be interwoven with the webbing already done, as in weaving.

All webbing must be attached to the top of the seat frame except when springing a seat, then it is attached to the underside of the seat frame.

If the surface of the seat has a dip in it, you will need to pull the webbing across tightly from front to back as described. The woven webbing from side to side however must not be pulled too tightly otherwise the dip will disappear.

HESSIAN COVERING

Spring hessian is the strongest type of hessian to use. However on small "drop-in" seats a piece of 10oz hessian will be quite adequate.

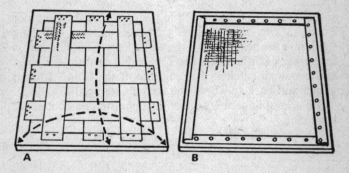

Fig. 9. *A*: Measure the seat at widest parts, *B*: Tack in place through the doubled hessian.

Measure across the seat at its widest part and add 50mm (2″) (see fig. 9A). Measure from front to back of the seat and add 50mm (2″). Cut a piece of hessian to the required size. Place the hessian over the webbing making sure the threads of the weave run straight from front to back and from side to side.

Fold the 25mm (1″) seam allowance all round the seat upwards. The hessian should just cover the webbing.

Tack in place through the doubled hessian with 13mm (½″) tacks placed approximately 40mm (1½″) apart (see fig. 9B).

BRIDLES

The object of bridles is to hold the hair in place, therefore the tension of the bridles should be just loose enough to enable one to slide one's flattened hand and hair underneath a bridle (i.e. a long tacking stitch).

Take enough twine to go round the seat and thread a half circular needle. Starting in the front right hand corner 75mm (3″) in from each edge, make a stitch 25mm (1″) long in the hessian. Do not catch the webbing (see fig. 10A). Make an upholsterer's knot (see page 26).

Make a long tacking stitch to the back right-hand corner 75mm (3″) in from each edge, make a 25mm (1″) long stitch into the hessian; do not make a knot. Continue across to the back left-hand corner 75mm (3″) in from the edge, make a small stitch as before, ditto at the front left-hand corner and back to where you started (see fig. 10B).

Tie a knot to secure against the upholsterer's knot at the beginning.

If you have an oblong seat, make two stitches along both long sides.

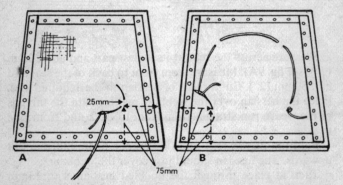

Fig. 10. *A*: First stitch for bridles, *B*: The next three corners.

FILLING THE BRIDLES

Having washed the hair (see page 26) or bought new stuffing, pick the stuffing over carefully teasing out any lumps. Do this by holding a small quantity of hair in your left hand and pulling small tufts of hair with your right hand from your left hand. Be sure to tease out all small knots or lumps.

Place small portions of the hair or stuffing in the palm of your hand (see fig. 11A) and push part way under the bridles from the middle of the seat outwards towards the edge. The edge of the hair should come two thirds of the way out between the bridles and the edge of the chair (see fig. 11B).

Start by stuffing at the back of the seat and work your way round. If there is a hollow in the centre of the seat, fill this up with more stuffing.

Keep the hair flat on the palm of your hand with all the ends of the hair laying flat. Do not fold the hair in at the edges or curl into a ball before putting under the bridles as these bent edges will feel uncomfortable in the seat.

Keep the stuffing evenly distributed and fairly tightly

Fig. 11.   Filling the bridles, *A*: Take small portions of hair / stuffing, *B*: Push part way under the bridles, *C*: Feel for unevenness.

packed. It is only from experience that one learns the correct
amount of stuffing to use in a seat, but for a small drop-in
seat the amount of stuffing to be used is small. Sufficient to
give a rounded effect, remembering that hair condenses to
less than half the height that it is now; so do pack the hair
fairly tightly. The same applies to other fillings.

Having stuffed the bridles, feel for any unevenness in the
stuffing. With your eyes closed and your fingers curled as
for playing the piano, feel for lumps and hollows. Rectify
where necessary, teasing out lumps and filling hollows (see
fig. 11C).

WADDING

Measure from the outside top edge of the side frame of
your chair seat over the stuffing to the other side at the
widest part. Do not allow extra for turnings (see fig. 12A).

Measure from the front to the back over the stuffing,
taking the measurement from the top outside edge of the
frame. Do not allow any extra for turnings.

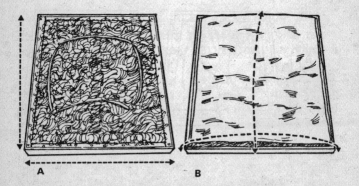

Fig. 12. How to measure, A: For the wadding, B: For the
calico cover add 50mm (2in).

The wadding will expand and will need to be trimmed back as the calico flattens the wadding when being pulled tightly over the seat.

The wadding must go as far as the outside edge of the frame under the calico but never down the sides because the drop-in seat probably wouldn't drop in the chair frame if it did.

Cut, tear or pull apart a piece of wadding or similar to the required size.

Place the wadding over the top of the stuffing, keeping the back edge parallel with the back of the frame. Tear the wadding to fit up to the edges all round the seat frame.

The reason for the wadding being put on top of the stuffing is to stop the small fibres working their way through to the top cover and feeling prickly against one's legs!

CALICO COVER

Measure from the bottom of the seat rail on one side, over the top of the seat and down to the bottom edge of the other side of the rail at the widest part. Add 50mm (2″) for turnings to go round to the bottom of the seat (see fig. 12B).

Measure from the front to the back of your seat frame in the same way and add 50mm (2″).

Cut a piece of calico, curtain lining, sheeting or a similar new strongly woven fabric to size. Lay the calico centrally over the seat. As the calico is a strongly-woven fabric it is not necesary to turn under the edge, and indeed is far easier not to.

Temporarily tack the calico with 13mm (½″) tacks to the underside of the seat frame at the back. Stop 50mm (2″) from the corners (see fig. 13A). *N.B. Temporary tack* – drive the tacks into the wood halfway only, you may well want to take them out later.

Stand the frame on its back edge, holding the frame up against yourself, pull the calico upwards and forwards to the front of the seat. The calico must be pulled forward as tightly as possible. This is best done by running the knuckle

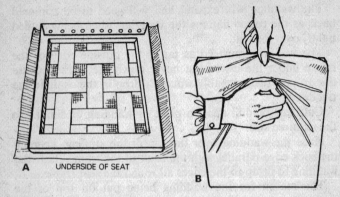

Fig. 13. *A*: **Temporarily tack calico to underside of seat,** *B*: **Stretching the calico.**

of your right hand thumb up the centre of the seat from back to front and at the same time pulling the calico upwards and forwards with your left hand (see fig. 13B). Drive in a temporary tack to attach the calico to the underside of the seat frame. Obviously you will have to lay the frame upside down, still holding the calico tightly, to drive in the tack. There is no need to turn under a hem when attaching the calico.

Pull the calico forward in this way for every tack. Work outwards from the centre tack stopping 50mm (2″) away from each corner.

By working the calico forward with one's thumb knuckle the wadding underneath will be flattened, stretched and brought forward. Make sure that the wadding is still centrally over the stuffing and that the frame edge cannot be felt through the calico. Make sure also that the wadding does not travel down the sides of the seat rail.

Attach the calico to the underside of the seat rail in the centre of each side with a temporary tack.

Pull the calico from the middle of the seat outwards and temporarily tack along both sides with 13mm ($\frac{1}{2}''$) tacks 40mm ($1\frac{1}{2}''$) apart stopping 50mm (2") away from each corner.

The corners: Take hold of the calico at its corner and pull round to the back of the seat frame. Place a tack to hold in position in the centre of the underside of the frame at the corner (see fig. 14A). Now tack along the sides or front or back into the corner making a mitre at each corner with the surplus fabric (see fig. 14B). Cut away the excess fabric on the inside of the fold, thus reducing the bulk. Drive in all temporary tacks.

The calico can be attached to the sides of the frame instead of underneath. In this case, make a neat fold at the corners to give a straight corner instead of a mitred corner, i.e. take hold of the calico from one side and pull it round the corner to the front of the seat frame and attach with a tack (see fig. 15A). Drive this tack in fully. Make a fold at the corner, cutting away excess fabric. Tack (see fig. 15B). Drive in all temporary tacks.

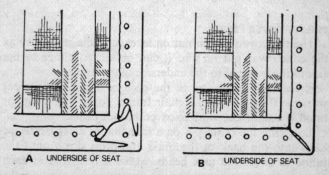

A UNDERSIDE OF SEAT   **B** UNDERSIDE OF SEAT

Fig. 14. A square corner where the calico is attached to the underside of the frame, *A*: Tack calico in position at corner, *B*: Tack along towards the corner and fold under to form a mitred corner.

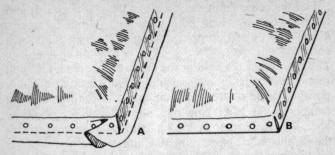

Fig. 15.   A square corner where the calico is attached to the sides of the frame. *A*: Pull the calico tightly round the corner and tack. *B*: Make a fold at the corner, cut away excess fabric and tack.

If you are working your pincushion seat straight onto the chair frame, pull the calico taut and place a tack at the corner. Pull the calico and tack, getting rid of all the excess fabric and making sure the calico lays flat with no wrinkles (see fig. 16).

THE TOP COVER FABRIC

The top cover will be put on in exactly the same way as the calico was put on and it can be tacked either to the side of the frame or to the underside of the frame.

If the tacks show, as in the case of a pincushion seat worked straight onto the chair frame, cover with gimp or braid of a sufficient width to cover the tack heads.

To attach the braid put on a thin film of clear Bostik or Uhu onto the back of the braid and press down onto the fabric to cover the tack heads. Make a neat fold at each corner. Cover the first end of the braid by placing the folded other end on top.

Drive in a matching coloured gimp pin at each corner and two others spaced evenly on each side.

Finally tack a piece of black cloth, hessian, calico or similar over the underside of the seat, to act as a dust cover and to cover up all the workings of your seat.

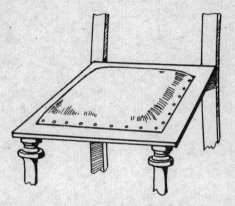

Fig. 16. Calico tacked straight onto the chair frame.

2

DROP-IN PINCUSHION SEAT
(FOAM UPHOLSTERY)

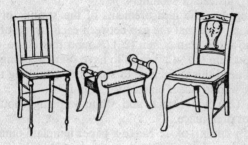

SHOPPING LIST

... m/yds webbing
... x ... 2″ thick foam
... x ... 1″ thick foam
16mm ($\frac{5}{8}$″) tacks

13mm ($\frac{1}{2}$″) tacks

... m/yds calico
... m/yds top cover fabric
... m/yds braid
... m/yds black cloth
(optional)
Adhesive (i.e. Uhu, Bostik, etc.)

Take the drop-in seat out of the stool or chair frame. Turn it upside down.

If there is a piece of black cloth or similar fabric tacked to the bottom of your frame covering the underside of the webbing, remove this fabric so you can see the webbing. There is no need to remove any more of the old upholstery materials before measuring.

If your chair has a pincushion seat but no drop-in frame, measure in the same way but turn the whole chair upside down.

WEBBING: Measure that part of the webbing that you can actually see and add 100mm (4″) to each length, i.e. 25mm (1″) at each end and hidden from view and 25mm (1″) for turnunders. For those chairs with no drop-in frame add 50mm (2″) instead of 100mm (4″).

Add together the measurements of the strands of webbing making sure that the gap between each strand of webbing is no more than 50mm (2″). Round this figure up by 250mm-300mm (10″-12″) so as to have some webbing over. You will need this to be able to stretch the webbing tightly round the web stretcher on the final strand.

50mm (2″) wide black and white webbing should be bought for preference.

50MM (2″) THICK FOAM: Make a paper template 6mm ($\frac{1}{4}$″) larger all round than the actual frame of the chair seat. Take this paper template with you, the shop keeper may well be kind and cut the foam to size and shape. The easiest way to do this is to place your drop-in seat on a large piece of paper and draw round the frame. Draw a second line 6mm ($\frac{1}{4}$″) outside the first line and cut round this second line.

If you have rather a small pincushion chair seat, you may find it would look better to use two thicknesses of 25mm (1″) thick foam instead of a 50mm (2″) piece and a 25mm (1″) piece.

25MM (1″) THICK FOAM: If you have a drop-in seat, cut a piece of 25mm (1″) thick foam 56mm (2$\frac{1}{4}$″) smaller all the way round than your paper pattern. Alternatively if you have no drop-in seat frame and your chair seat is not very big, then you can dispense with this doming piece of foam.

CALICO: You will need two pieces of calico plus four strips. One piece of calico must be 25mm (1″) larger all round than the seat frame and is used to go over the webbing and under the foam; the second piece of calico will go over the top of the foam and needs to be 100mm (4″) larger than the seat frame. The strips of calico must be 75mm (3″) wide by the length of each of the four edges of the frame. These will be used to hold the foam in place.

If you have no drop-in seat frame, you will need the two large pieces of calico only. You will not need the strips – the calico cover will hold the foam in place.

TERYLENE WADDING: The measurements for the terylene wadding will be the same as those for the 50mm (2″) thick piece of foam.

TOP COVER: The measurements for your top cover will be the same as those for the larger of the two pieces of calico.

BRAID OR GIMP: A drop-in seat will probably not need any braid. Braid is used solely to cover the heads of the tacks. With a drop-in seat all the tacks will be under the seat frame.

If you have no drop-in frame and you will be putting your tacks into the rebate on the chair, you must measure round the entire edge of the rebate. Allow 50mm (2″) extra for corners and the join.

BLACK CLOTH: Used only if you have a drop-in seat. This is optional, but it does act as a dust trap. The measurements will be the same as for the smaller piece of calico.

Having done your shopping and bought the necessary materials, start by gathering together all necessary tools.

If your chair has a drop-in seat, remove this from the chair frame. Turn to the Introduction on page 20 and read how to set about stripping your seat. Use furniture reviver if necessary before starting to re-upholster, see page 25.

Before starting to re-upholster your drop-in seat, check that the seat frame fits easily into the chair frame, remembering that both the calico and the final top cover will have to fit between the drop-in seat frame and the frame of the chair. Shave a little of the wood from the sides of the frame if necessary.

Incidentally the word "drop-in" means that your seat has been made up on a frame and dropped into the chair frame or stool frame when completed. "Pincushion" is the name given to the type of seat, i.e. like a pincushion with a rounded top.

WEBBING

Elasticated webbing – called "Pirelli" webbing is used to take the place of springs in modern upholstery, but in a small pincushion type seat, it is not necessary to have springs, therefore it is not necessary to have Pirelli webbing. Use traditional 50mm (2″) wide black and white webbing.

The method of attaching black and white webbing to a drop-in seat is explained on page 32. Follow these instructions until all the webbing is completed in both directions. Then return to this page.

CALICO UNDER THE FOAM

It is necessary to put some material, such as calico or hessian between the webbing and the foam to stop the hard edges of the webbing cutting into the foam over the years during use. The procedure is similar to that given for hessian covering on page 35.

Measure across the widest part of the seat from the top of one outside edge to the other and add 50mm (2″) (see fig. 9A, page 35). Measure from front to back likewise and add 50mm (2″). Cut a piece of calico or similar to size.

Place the calico over the webbing making sure the threads of the weave run straight from front to back and from side to side. Fold the 25mm (1″) seam allowance all round the seat upwards. The calico should cover the webbing.

Tack in position through the doubled calico with 13mm ($\frac{1}{2}$″) tacks placed approximately 40mm ($1\frac{1}{2}$″) apart. This is the same procedure as for the hessian in fig. 9B, page 35.

FOAM

Using plain foam sheeting, you will need two pieces of foam, the larger piece cut from 50mm (2″) thick foam and the smaller piece for doming cut from 25mm (1″) thick foam.

Measure first for the smaller piece of foam, which will go under the larger piece to give the "domed" effect.

Measure from the top of the outside edge of the back of your seat frame to the outside front edge and deduct 100mm (4″) (see fig. 17A). Measure likewise from one outside edge across to the other outside edge of the seat frame and deduct 100mm (4″). Cut a piece of 25mm (1″) thick foam to size.

"Feather" the edges. Take a pair of scissors and cut away a 20mm (¾″) triangle from the entire bottom edge of the block of foam (see fig. 17B).

Measure from the outside top edge of the back of your seat frame to the outside top front edge and add 13mm (½″). Measure likewise from one side of the frame across to the other side and add 13mm (½″). Cut a piece of 50mm (2″) thick foam to size. Feather the edges as before by cutting away a 25mm (1″) triangle from the entire bottom edge of the block of foam. You may find it easier to use a serrated knife as this time you will be cutting away a larger piece of foam.

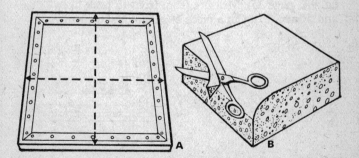

Fig. 17. A: Measuring for the 25mm (1in thick) foam, B: Feathering the 25mm (1in thick) foam.

It is important to feather tidily on this larger piece of foam leaving a smooth clean edge along the outside edge of the foam.

The bottom of the block of foam will now be smaller than the seat frame with the top edge overhanging the frame by 6mm ($\frac{1}{4}''$) all round.

If you are working on a drop-in seat tear four strips of calico, one of the length of each of the four sides by approximately 75mm (3″) deep. Do not cut the calico with scissors as the resulting hard line may show through the top cover.

Stick the strips of calico to the top of the foam with adhesive such as Uhu, Bostik or Copydex (see fig. 18A). Squeeze the adhesive from the tube in a long thickish line down the long edge of a piece of calico. Do likewise along one top edge of the foam. Place the strip of calico along the sticky top edge of one side of the foam. Leave to dry completely.

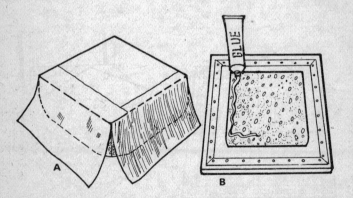

Fig. 18. *A*: Stick the calico strips to the top of the 50mm (2in thick) foam, *B*: Squeeze a line of adhesive around the top edges of the smaller piece of 25mm (1in thick) foam.

Meanwhile place the smaller 25mm (1") thick piece of foam onto the centre of your chair seat and squeeze a line of adhesive round the top edges, so it will stick to the other pieces of foam, shortly to be placed on top of it (see fig. 18B).

Centre the 50mm (2") thick foam on top of the 25mm (1") foam and temporarily tack the calico strips with 13mm tacks to the sides of the frame.

You should now have a nicely rounded edge to the side of your seat and a nice domed effect to the seat itself (see fig. 19A).

Drive in all temporary tacks when you are satisfied that they are in the correct position.

If you are working a pincushion seat directly onto your chair frame, and the rebate is small, the fewer tacks you use the better. Therefore measure and cut the 50mm (2") thick piece of foam as above and feather it, but do not stick strips of calico to the foam (see fig. 19B). The foam will be held in place by the calico cover.

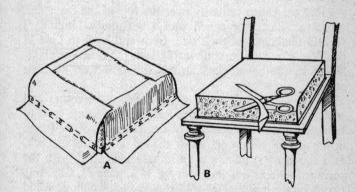

Fig. 19. A: Temporarily tack the calico strips to the side of the frame, B: Work a pin-cushion seat directly onto the chair frame. Carefully feather the top edges.

Unless you have a large pincushion seat one piece of 50mm (2″) thick foam should be sufficient for your seat without adding a second smaller piece for doming.

TERYLENE WADDING

It is not absolutely necessary to cover the foam with terylene wadding, but the finished effect will be nicer.

Measure across the top of the foam at the widest part of the seat from one outside edge to the other outside edge. Measure likewise from the outside front edge to the outside back edge, measuring over across the top of the foam. Cut a piece of terylene wadding to size. Lay the wadding centrally over the top of the foam.

CALICO

Measure across the top of the foam and wadding at the widest part of the seat from one outside edge to the other outside edge and add 50mm (2″). Measure likewise from the outside front edge to the outside back edge over the top of the foam and wadding and add 50mm (2″). Cut a piece of calico to size.

Place the calico centrally over the top of the foam and wadding. Attach the calico with a temporary 13mm ($\frac{1}{2}$″) tack in the centre of each side, front and back to hold in position. Continue to temporarily tack the calico in place. There should be no slack in the calico and no wrinkles either.

The corners: Take hold of the calico at its corner and pull round to the back of the seat frame. Place a tack to hold in position in the centre of the underside of the frame at the corner. Now work along the sides, or front or back, into the corner making a mitre at each corner with the surplus fabric as was shown in fig. 14A, page 41. Cut away excess on the inside of the fold, thus reducing bulk. Drive in all temporary tacks.

If you are working your pincushion seat straight onto the chair frame, pull the calico taut and place a tack at the corner. Pull the calico and tack, getting rid of all the excess fabric and making sure the calico lays flat with no wrinkles (see fig. 20).

THE TOP COVER

The top cover will be put on in exactly the same way as the calico was put on and it can be tacked either to the side of the frame or to the underside of the frame.

If the tacks show, as in the case of a pincushion seat worked straight onto the chair frame, cover with braid or gimp of a sufficient width to cover the tack heads.

To attach the braid, put a thin film of clear Bostik or Uhu onto the back of the braid and press down onto the fabric to cover the tack heads. Make a neat mitred fold at each corner. Cover the first end of the braid by placing the folded other end on top.

Drive in a matching coloured gimp pin at each corner and two others spaced evenly on each side. If you cannot buy gimp pins to match, they can easily be coloured by either painting with a paintbrush or putting into a small pot of enamel paint.

Finally tack a piece of black cloth, hessian, calico or similar over the underside of the seat, to act as a dust cover and to cover up all the tack heads.

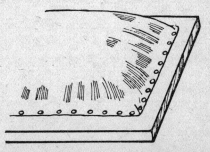

Fig. 20. Tacking straight onto the chair frame.

3

OTTOMAN
(OR SEAT WITH ROLLED EDGE AND PADDED TOP)

(TRADITIONAL UPHOLSTERY)

SHOPPING LIST

For the seat
... m/yds webbing –
if necessary
... m/yds hessian
... lbs stuffing
... m/yds cotton wadding
... m/yds calico
... m/yds top cover fabric
... m/yds braid –
if necessary
16mm ($\frac{5}{8}$") tacks for webbing
13mm ($\frac{1}{2}$") tacks
Gimp pins
Twine

Ottoman's base
... m/yds terylene wadding
... m/yds cord for holding the
lid in an upright position
... m/yds lining fabric
... m/yds top cover fabric
Staple gun and staples –
optional
Adhesive for braid

Take the measurements for your shopping list before stripping your Ottoman or chair/stool seat, if it is upholstered already. If you are upholstering an Ottoman take the measurements of both the base and the seat, however if you are upholstering a chair or stool, then measure for the seat only.

FOR THE SEAT

Ottomans generally have a solid base to their lids; if yours is upholstered feel through the lining under the lid and check if this is so. If it is you will not need webbing. If you can feel or see a frame then measure for webbing and a piece of hessian to cover.

WEBBING: Measure the length of the stool seat (or Ottoman's lid) and add 50mm (2") to the measurement. Multiply by the number of webs needed, i.e. a 50mm (2") space and no more is needed between each 50mm (2") wide piece of webbing. Measure likewise across the seat, add 50mm (2") to each measurement and multiply by the number of webs needed. Add 250mm-300mm (10"-12") extra for tensioning the last web.

HESSIAN: You will need four strips of hessian 150mm (6") wide. Two should be the length of the front/back plus 50mm (2") and the other two should be the length of the sides plus 50mm (2").

If your seat is not on a solid wooden base, you will also need a piece of hessian to go over the entire frame, plus 25mm (1") turnings all round.

FIBRE: As a guide a piano stool measuring 18" x 12" will need approximately 2lbs of hair or fibre. An Ottoman will take approximately 4lbs, unless it is of a large size and has no stuffing on it already, then you will need extra.

COTTON WADDING: Measure over the top of the box from side to side and from front to back and, to be on the safe side, add 50mm (2") to each measurement to allow for the build up of the rolled edge and stuffing. Cotton wadding generally is bought from rolls 23" wide.

CALICO: As for the cotton wadding, but instead of 50mm (2″), add 100mm (4″) for seam allowance and to cover the roll and stuffing.

TOP COVER FABRIC: Measure across the top of the lid of the Ottoman or your stool/seat and add 50mm (2″) seam allowance for the width measurement. Measure likewise from back to front, adding 50mm (2″) for the length measurement.

OTTOMAN'S LINING FABRIC: Measure across the width of the inside of back panel, add on 50mm (2″). Measure the length of the inside back panel, base and inside front panel as one length. Add on sufficient to go over the top of the front and back panels and a further 50mm (2″) for seam allowance.

Measure across the width of both side panels. It may be that both sides can be got out of one width of fabric. Measure the length of the inside of the side panels, across the top of the side panels and add a further 75mm (3″) to each of the side panel length measurements.

Measure the length of the inside of the Ottoman's lid and add 50mm (2″). Measure the width and add 50mm (2″).

Make a plan if necessary showing how these four pieces of fabric will fit most economically into a width of fabric which is generally 48″ wide. Allow for pattern repeats if lining with a patterned fabric.

TERYLENE WADDING: Measure round all four sides in one piece by the height of the Ottoman's base. The straight of grain can run either up and down the Ottoman or across from side to side.

TOP COVER FABRIC: Measure across the outside of the front panel from side to side and add 50mm (2″) seam allowance to this width measurement. Measure the depth from the top of the front panel to the bottom and add 75mm (3″), being 25mm (1″) at the top and 50mm (2″) to go underneath the base. Repeat for all three other panels, i.e. the back and both sides.

Make a plan to show how these four pieces for the base

and the one piece from the lid will fit most economically into a width of fabric which is generally 48″ wide. Allow for pattern repeats.

TACKS: 4oz of 16mm ($\frac{5}{8}$″) tacks for attaching the webbing. 4oz of 13mm ($\frac{1}{2}$″) Upholsterer's tacks, not bayonet tacks.

TWINE: If you can't persuade an upholsterer or supplier to sell you a small hank of approximately twenty yards or so of upholsterer's twine, then use a really strong string which doesn't break easily.

ADHESIVE: Buy Clear Bostik or Uhu for attaching braid.

Having done your shopping and bought the necessary materials, gather up the tools needed for the next job which is to strip your stool or Ottoman if it is already upholstered. See the Introduction on page 20 and don't forget to give the wood some attention before upholstering, see page 25.

If you have a stool to upholster, please turn to page 62 and follow instructions as for upholstering the lid of the Ottoman.

To make an Ottoman, use a strong wooden box with a wooden lid, which then can be made into an ideal blanket box, sewing box, piano stool, child's toy box, etc. There are many uses for such a nicely covered box.

Take the box, inspect for strength and woodworm; if possible remove the lid for easier upholstering and start by upholstering the container or bottom part of the box.

For putting on the lining, it is usually easier to use a staple gun but if you haven't got one, don't buy one specially. Use your hammer and tacks. However, if using tacks, check that the wood is thick enough to take the whole tack and that the point does not appear on the other side. Should this happen, use a 10mm tack or smaller.

LINING THE INSIDE OF YOUR OTTOMAN

Cut out all four pieces of fabric first.

For the length of fabric required for the first piece of

lining, measure across the top of the back panel, down the inside of the back panel, across the bottom of the Ottoman, up the inside front panel and over its top (see fig. 21A, A1). Add 50mm (2″) to this measurement for seam allowance.

For the width, measure across the top of the inside front panel – or should the box not be in the form of a square or oblong, then measure across at its widest part. Add 50mm (2″) seam allowance. Cut a piece of lining fabric to size, remembering that the straight of grain should run from the top of the Ottoman down towards the bottom.

For the length measurement for the other two side panel pieces, measure across the top of the side panel and down the inside (see fig. 21A, A2). Add 75mm (3″) to this measurement for seam allowance. For the width, measure across the top of the side panel and add 50mm (2″) seam allowance. Cut two pieces of lining fabric to size.

Measure the depth from front to back of the lid and add 50mm (2″) to this measurement. Do likewise, add 50mm (2″) to the width measurement.

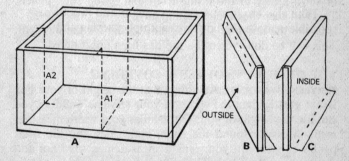

Fig. 21. *A*: Where to measure the length for the first piece of lining (A1) and for the side panels (A2), *B*: Staple the lining from the outside, *C*: Staple lining to bottom panel.

Starting with one of the two side panels, staple or tack with 13mm ($\frac{1}{2}$″) tacks one end of the length over onto the outside of a side panel, allowing the fabric to fall 25mm (1″) over the side (see fig. 21B). Keep the staples or tacks 13mm ($\frac{1}{2}$″) down from the top of the panel. Smooth the lining over the top and down the inside of the side panel (see fig. 21C) and staple or tack to the bottom panel. Take care to see that the lining is tucked well into the corners. Staple all raw edges on either side to the front and back panels as appropriate, 13mm ($\frac{1}{2}$″) in from the corners. The staples or tacks will then be covered by the lining running in the opposite direction. Repeat with the other side panel.

The long piece of lining must now be tacked or stapled to the outside of the back panel, allowing 25mm (1″) to fall over the back. Cut the fabric in the four places at each side of the lid's two hinges, if appropriate, so that the lining fits snugly round the hinges. Smooth the lining over the top of the back panel, down inside the back panel, across the Ottoman's base, up inside the front panel and attach 13mm ($\frac{1}{2}$″) down from the top of the front panel to the outside of the front panel. At the same time turn under both side edges.

These edges can either be ladder stitched (see page 100) or sewn neatly to the inside front and inside back panels. This will keep the lining taut and tidy.

Leave the lining of the inside of the lid for the moment. This will be done when the top has been upholstered.

THE OTTOMAN'S OUTSIDE COVERING

TERYLENE WADDING: Assuming that the height of your box is not greater than the width of your terylene wadding you can use the height of your Ottoman as your width measurement. Measure round the back, both sides and the front panels to give you your length measurement. Do not add on a seam allowance. The terylene wadding ends will lie side by side at the join. Cut the terylene wadding (or similar) to size and attach it to the outside of the Ottoman. It is only necessary to put the odd tack or staple in to hold in place until the top cover is put on.

Tack or staple every 50mm (2″) down the length of the "join" which should be at the back of the Ottoman. The two ends of the terylene wadding should abut and not overlap.

TOP COVER FABRIC: There is no need to use a calico cover before putting on the top cover on the sides of the Ottoman.

Measure each of the four panels separately remembering that the grain of the fabric must run from the top of the box down to the bottom for the top cover fabric. You must also centre any pattern. Add 50mm (2″) to each width measurement and 75mm (3″) to each length measurement for seam allowance. Cut to size.

Starting in the centre of the back panel "back-tack" the material to the panel at the top edge. To back-tack, see fig. 22A. Cut several strips of cardboard; a cereal box is ideal. These should be as long as you can cut them by 13mm (½″) wide. With the right side of the fabric facing the back panel

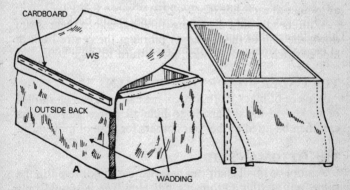

Fig. 22.   A: Back-tacking, B: For side panels, turn the seam allowance under at both sides.

of the Ottoman, cover the top 25mm (1″) of the panel. The rest of the fabric will be standing up in the air (or more likely falling into the box!).

Leaving 25mm (1″) seam allowance on the side edge uncardboarded, place a strip of cardboard on top of the top cover fabric and wadding along and exactly flush with, the top edge of the back panel. Tack with 13mm (½″) tacks or staple through the cardboard, top cover fabric and wadding onto the back panel of the Ottoman. You will find it easier to put in the odd temporary tack or staple here and there to hold both pieces of fabric and cardboard in position. When you are satisfied that the top edge is level with the top edge of the Ottoman, tack or staple at 50mm (2″) intervals.

Take the top cover fabric round to the side panels and tack down the edge with 13mm (½″) tacks placed 75mm (3″) apart.

Smooth the top cover down to the bottom of each panel, and attach with staples or 13mm (½″) tacks to the underside of the Ottoman.

Work the front panel as for the back panel. The side panels are worked in the same way, but turn under the seam allowance at each side (see fig. 22B).

With needle and matching thread make a neat seam down the join of the top cover fabric at the centre back in ladder stitch. For directions, please turn to page 100.

THE UNDERSIDE OF THE OTTOMAN

A piece of black cloth, calico, hessian, etc. can be stapled or tacked to the underside to hide all raw edges. Castors can then be fitted to the four corners for ease of movement.

THE OTTOMAN'S LID

A stool or small chair can have its seat upholstered in the same way as this Ottoman's lid. However it should only be used for small seating areas, as this type of seat is not so strong or long lasting as, for instance, an unsprung seat.

Assuming your Ottoman has a solid wooden lid, you will make a "roll" round the edge to keep the stuffing on the top of the Ottoman in place and to ensure the lid edge will be strong and firm in use.

If your Ottoman's lid is made as a frame and therefore is not "solid", then it must first be webbed and a piece of hessian tacked to the top of the lid to cover the hole(s). Please turn back to page 32 and follow the instructions for webbing and attaching the hessian for a pincushion seat.

THE ROLL

Measure the length of the front of the lid and add 50mm (2"). Cut a strip of 150mm (6") wide hessian by the required length. Cut three more strips of 150mm (6") wide hessian for both sides and the back of the lid. If your seat is round or kidney shaped, then cut strips of hessian to go round the seat, one piece overlapping the next by 25mm (1").

Using 13mm (½") tacks attach the long edge of the strip of hessian along the entire front of the lid tacking as close to the front edge of the lid as possible, so that 130mm (5") of the hessian will fall over to the front of the Ottoman (see fig. 23A). Take some hair or fibre so as to make a long well-compacted roll the thickness of a sausage (not chipolata!)

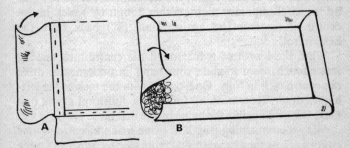

Fig. 23.   A: Tack the hessian along the edges, B: The roll with mitred corners.

and the entire length of the front of the lid. Fold the hessian right round this roll of hair, tucking the surplus hessian well underneath. This roll needs to be made very firm and tightly packed and you must not be able to bend it at all.

Using 13mm ($\frac{1}{2}''$) tacks attach this roll as near to the first row of tacks as possible, stopping 40mm ($1\frac{1}{2}''$) from either end. The edge of the roll should be flush with the edge of the lid. Leave the ends of the hessian for the moment, these will be mitred when all four rolled edges have been worked. A round or kidney shaped stool of course will not have mitred corners.

Repeat with the back and both sides.

Mitre each corner by turning the hessian inwards at a 45° angle from the corner. Tack to make neat and straight corners (see fig. 23B).

THE BRIDLES

Assuming your Ottoman's lid is made of solid wood, take a piece of twine the length being one and a half times round the circumference of the lid.

Tie a knot 40mm ($1\frac{1}{2}''$) in from one end of the twine, and attach this with a 13mm ($\frac{1}{2}''$) tack near the front right-hand corner, measured 75mm (3") in from each of the hessian rolls. Temporary tack a 13mm ($\frac{1}{2}''$) tack 75mm (3") in each way from the hessian roll at the left-hand front corner (see fig. 24A). Temporary tack another 13mm ($\frac{1}{2}''$) tack in the centre of the front lid again 75mm (3") back from the hessian roll.

Wind the length of twine round the centre tack leaving just enough room to slide your hand in underneath, drive the centre tack in fully. Do likewise with the tack at the left-hand corner. Repeat on all four sides, finish off at the first tack, tying off against the twine by the first tack.

With the remaining length of twine make a centre row of bridles across the Ottoman's lid from side to side using three tacks.

If your Ottoman has a wooden frame as the base of its

lid, work the bridles as for a drop-in seat, see page 36. The same applies to stools and chairs with webbing and hessian on their base frames.

FILLING THE BRIDLES

Having washed the hair (see page 26) or bought new stuffing, pick the stuffing over carefully teasing out any lumps. Do this by holding a small quantity of hair in your left hand and pulling small tufts of hair with your right hand from your left hand. Be sure to tease out all small knots and lumps.

Place small portions of the hair or stuffing in the palm of your hand and push partway under the bridles from the middle of the seat outwards towards the hessian roll at the edge. The edge of the hair should come right up against the edge of the roll (see fig. 24B). Start by stuffing at the back of the seat and work your way round.

Keep the stuffing flat on the palm of your hand with all the ends of the hair or stuffing laying flat. Do not fold the stuffing in at the edges or curl into a ball before putting under the bridles as these bent edges will feel uncomfort-

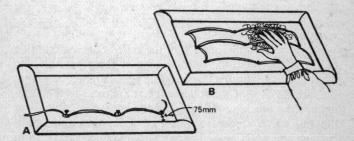

Fig. 24. *A*: Attaching the bridles, *B*: Push hair under bridles.

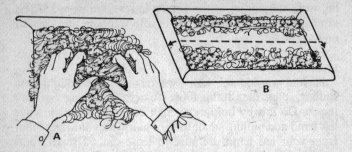

Fig. 25. *A*: Feel for unevenness, *B*: Measure for the wadding.

able in the seat. Keep the stuffing evenly distributed and fairly tightly packed.

It is only from experience that one learns the correct amount of stuffing to use, but the stuffing does need to be fairly tightly packed and will compress to less than half the height it was before.

Having stuffed the bridles, feel for any unevenness in the stuffing. With your eyes closed and your fingers curled as for playing the piano, feel for lumps and hollows. Rectify where necessary, teasing out lumps and filling hollows (see fig. 25A).

WADDING

Measure from the outside of the rolled edge on one side of the Ottoman to the outside edge of the other side. No need to allow extra for turnings (see fig. 25B). Measure from the outside edge of the rolled edge at the front of the Otto-man to the outside rolled edge at the back, measuring over the stuffing. No need to allow extra for turnings, this is because the wadding will expand and will need to be trim-med back as the calico flattens the wadding when being pulled tightly over the Ottoman.

The wadding must go as far as the bottom of the outside edge of the rolled edge under the calico but never round underneath the lid or chair/stool seat.

Cut, tear or pull apart a piece of wadding or similar to the required size.

Place the wadding over the top of the stuffing, keeping the back edge parallel with the back of the frame. Tear the wadding to fit over the rolled edge all round the other three sides.

The reason for putting wadding on top of the stuffing is to stop the stuffing fibres working their way through to the top cover.

CALICO COVER

Measure from the front of your Ottoman's lid or chair/stool seat to the back and add 50mm (2") to this measurement. Measure likewise from side to side and add 50mm (2") to this measurement. Cut a piece of calico, curtain lining, sheeting or similar new strongly woven fabric to size.

Place the calico centrally over the lid/seat. As the calico is a strongly woven material it is not necessary to turn under the seam allowance at the edges and indeed it is far easier not to.

Using 13mm ($\frac{1}{2}$") tacks temporarily tack the calico to the underside of the lid. On a chair/stool this may not be possible, therefore tack to the outside of the back of the seat. See that the wadding covers the roll and frame completely. Tack to within 75mm (3") of the corners.

Pull the calico forward to the front edge of the front of the lid and temporary tack to the underside of the lid. This calico must be pulled forward as tightly as possible. This is probably best done by running the knuckle of your right hand across the lid from back to front and at the same time pulling the calico forward with your left hand (see fig. 26A). Still holding the calico firmly, drive in a temporary tack in the unfolded calico on the underside of the lid (see fig. 26B).

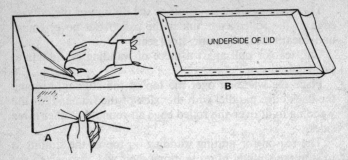

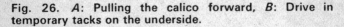

Fig. 26. *A*: Pulling the calico forward, *B*: Drive in temporary tacks on the underside.

Pull the calico forward in this way for every tack, working outwards from the centre tack and stopping 75mm (3″) from each corner. As you attach the calico with more tacks, the first tacks holding the calico to the centre front, can be taken out and re-fixed pulling the calico more tightly.

By working the calico forward with one's thumb knuckle the wadding underneath will be flattened and brought forward. Make sure that the wadding is now centrally over the stuffing and that the frame cannot be felt through the calico.

Attach the calico in the centre of each side with a temporary tack. Pull the calico from the middle of the lid outwards and temporarily tack with 13mm ($\frac{1}{2}$″) tacks 40mm (1$\frac{1}{2}$″) apart, along the entire length of the sides.

OTTOMAN'S CORNERS: Take hold of the calico in its own corner, pull tightly and attach with a tack to the underside of the lid in a line with the other tacks (see fig. 14). Finish off attaching the calico and fold under the excess at the corners. Repeat with all corners. Drive home all temporary tacks.

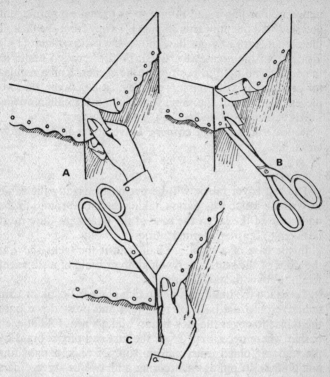

Fig. 27. *A*: Pull calico hard round corner and tack, *B*: Cut away surplus calico, *C*: Run scissors up crease, at same time pulling calico downwards tightly to get a square corner.

CHAIR/STOOL CORNERS: Pull the calico hard round the corner horizontally and then very slightly downwards. Drive in a tack fully (see fig. 27A). Fold the calico to make a straight line vertically exactly at the corner. Run the calico between your finger and thumb so as to make a permanent crease. Cut a line upwards 25mm (1″) away from the tack at the corner, turn and cut back down the calico 40mm (1½″) inside from the crease (fig. 27B). Fold the calico under at the crease and hold in position at the corner. Run a regulator or points of your scissors up the crease between the two pieces of calico, at the same time pulling the calico downwards very tightly (see fig. 27C). Tack in position.

Repeat for the other corners. Drive home all temporary tacks.

TOP COVER

The top cover fabric will be put on in exactly the same way as the calico was put on, taking the fabric round to the underside of the lid in the case of the Ottoman. Care must be taken to centre patterned fabrics.

In the case of a stool or chair seat, if the tacks show at the sides of the seat, cover with gimp or braid of a sufficient width to cover the tack heads.

To attach the braid, put a thin film of clear Bostik or Uhu adhesive onto the back of the braid and press down onto the fabric to cover the tack heads. Make a neat fold at each corner where necessary. Cover the first end of the braid by placing the folded other end on top. Drive in a matching coloured gimp pin at each corner and two or three others spaced evenly in between.

If you cannot buy gimp pins to match, they can easily be coloured by either painting with a paintbrush or putting into a small pot of enamel paint.

The Ottoman's lid must be finished off by attaching a piece of the lining fabric to the underside of the lid. Measure across the top of the lid and add 50mm (2″) for the tuck-unders. Measure likewise from back to front of the lid adding 50mm (2″). Cut a piece of lining fabric to size. Turn under the seam allowances and pin to the underside of the lid. Neatly stitch with ladder stitch.

If the lid was taken off the base of the Ottoman to make upholstery easier, refix it and attach cords at both sides to prevent the lid opening too far.

4

UNSPRUNG SEAT
(TRADITIONAL UPHOLSTERY)

SHOPPING LIST

... m/yds webbing
... m/yds hessian
... m/yds scrim
... lbs stuffing
... m/yds wadding
16mm tacks
13mm tacks

... m/yds calico
... m/yds top cover fabric
... m/yds braid
... m/yds black cloth –
                 optional
Twine
Adhesive

It is being assumed that it is the seat only of your chair or sofa that will need to be re-upholstered. It is quite probable that the back and/or arms will only need recovering with a little padding added. Therefore allow cotton wadding and calico for the inside of the back and arms only, but measure both inside back and outside back – also inside and outside arms if appropriate – as well as the seat when calculating the amount of top cover fabric needed. The braid measurements also will need adjusting. (See chapter 7 – top cover for a wing-backed chair.)

You can take the measurements for your shopping list before you start to strip your chair.

Turn your chair upside down. If there is black cloth or similar tacked to the bottom you may find it easier to remove it so that you can see the webbing.

WEBBING: Measure that part of each length of webbing that you can actually see, add 100mm (4″) to each length, i.e. 25mm (1″) at each end which is hidden from view and 25mm (1″) for turnunders. Add up the measurements of the strands of webbing and add 250mm-300mm (10″-12″) so that you will be able to have enough webbing for stretching the final web.

Make sure the gap between each strand of webbing is no more than 50mm (2″). If the gaps between the webbing on your chair are larger than 50mm (2″), measure for an extra strand of webbing. 50mm (2″) wide black and white webbing is the ideal webbing to use.

HESSIAN: Measure the length and the width of the underpart of the seat and add on 100mm (4″) to each measurement for turnunders. It is usually worth buying 12oz hessian in preference to 10oz as it is that much stronger.

SCRIM: Measure loosely over the top of the chair seat from side to side, including both outside edges and add 50mm (2″) for turnings. Measure over the top from the back to the front of the seat including the back outside edge and the front outside edge and add 50mm (2″) for turnings.

If you have any difficulty in obtaining scrim, use 10oz hessian instead. In that case buy 10oz hessian to cover the webbing and very often it is possible to get both pieces out side by side from a 72″ wide hessian.

STUFFING: If there is horse hair in your chair, wash and re-use it. To discover if there is horse hair in your chair before stripping, turn your chair upside down and you will see some of the hair fibres beginning to poke out through the hessian.

If there is no horse hair in your chair, buy hair, black fibre or curly coir. 2-2½lbs should be sufficient for a dining-room chair seat. You will need double that for a small arm-chair seat.

COTTON WADDING: Measure the length and width over the top of the seat, including the outside edges. There is no need to add a turnunder allowance. Cotton wadding is generally sold from a roll 23" wide. Alternatively, buy a terylene wadding. Add extra for back and arms if necessary.

CALICO: Measure as for the cotton wadding but add 150mm (6") to each measurement for seam allowance and for the possibility that you may build up your chair seat to be larger than the existing one. Allow extra for back and arms if necessary.

TOP COVER FABRIC: Measure over the existing top cover and add 75mm (3") all round to be sure of having enough fabric – seats do alter their shape when re-upholstered! It can be to your advantage to complete the job of upholstering your chair before buying the fabric for the top cover. Allow extra for back and arms if necessary.

BRAID: If there is braid on your chair already, measure all the braid and allow a little extra for corners and turnings. If there is no braid on your chair and there should be, then measure all the way round the chair seat, add a little extra for corners and turnings.

Sometimes there will be no show-wood on the chair seat and the top cover fabric will be taken right down the sides of the chair and fastened underneath the chair, in which case there is no need for braid. The only reason for having braid is to cover the tack heads.

BLACK CLOTH: Measure underneath the chair seat and add 50mm (2") to both the length and width for turnunders. The reason for the black cloth is that it acts as a dust cover. Not all chairs have black cloth and you can just as easily use some pieces of left-over hessian. You can even sew two pieces of hessian together to make one piece that is big enough to fit under your chair.

TACKS: 4oz of 16mm and 6oz of 13mm upholsterer's tacks, not bayonet tacks. However if the wood on the top of your frame is only 25mm (1″) or so wide, it would be safer and less likely to split the wood if you were to use 13mm ($\frac{1}{2}$″) tacks instead of the 16mm ($\frac{5}{8}$″) tacks for the webbing. Likewise drop down one size and use 10mm ($\frac{3}{8}$″) instead of of 13mm ($\frac{1}{2}$″) tacks for the hessian and calico, etc.

TWINE: As upholsterer's twine comes in rather a big and expensive ball, try to persuade an upholsterer to sell you a small quantity; some sell small hanks of approximately 20 yards. It is well worth while to buy the real thing; for a start it is so much easier to work with and for another it is stronger.

Having done your shopping and bought the necessary materials, gather up your tools needed for the next job which is "stripping and preparing the frame", see page 20.

If you are upholstering the seat of a hall sofa, leave the top cover on the curved inside back so as to keep the present upholstery undisturbed until you are ready to put on the new top cover fabric. The same applies to a chair with arms.

WEBBING

16mm ($\frac{5}{8}$″) improved tacks should be used for attaching 50mm (2″) wide black and white webbing to the seat.

Because your chair is to have no springs in the seat, the webbing should be attached to the top of the seat rail. The strands of webbing should be spaced evenly over the seat, and the space between each piece of webbing should not be wider than the width of the webbing to be used (see fig. 28A).

With a pencil, mark on the top of the front seat rail where the webbing will come. Do the same with the back rail. If

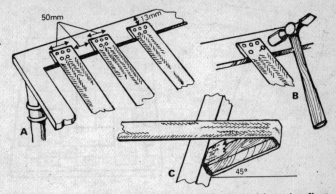

Fig. 28. *A*: Spacing the webbing, *B*: Attaching the first web, *C*: Tensioning the webbing at the other end.

the back rail is shorter than the front rail, the webs will be slightly closer together at the back. Do the same on the top of each side rail.

Take your roll of webbing, turn under 25mm (1″) and place the fold 13mm (½″) back in from the outside edge of the seat rail at the back of your chair. Secure with five 16mm (⅝″) tacks in the formation as shown in figure 28B.

You must attach the webbing to the other side of the frame under tension. Wind the webbing over the top of your piece of wood (or use a web stretcher), back underneath the wood and up to cover the end nearest the seat rail, with the webbing pulled fairly taut over the wood and the wood at a slight upward angle (see fig. 28C).

Tighten the webbing by pressing downwards on the wooden stretcher until it is at the parallel with the seat rail. Put in three 16mm (⅝″) tacks in a straight line, one at each corner and one in the middle, 13mm (½″) back in from the outside edge of the seat rail. Cut the webbing, leaving 50mm (2″) clear from the tacks.

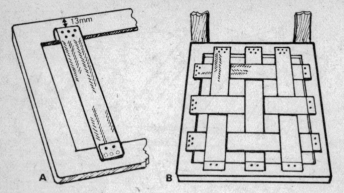

Fig. 29. *A*: Drive in the last two tacks, *B*: Webbing must be interlaced.

Turn the webbing over and drive in two more 16mm ($\frac{5}{8}''$) tacks in a position between the three tacks already holding the webbing and slightly forward of them (see fig. 29A).

Complete all the webbing in one direction first before starting to web in the other direction.

When webbing your seat in the other direction, it must be interlaced as when weaving (see fig. 29B).

HESSIAN COVER

Measure from the top of one side of the seat rail to the top of the other side of the seat rail at the widest point and add 50mm (2") to this measurement (see fig. 30A). Measure likewise from the back of the seat to the front of the seat, and add 50mm (2") to this measurement also.

Cut a piece of hessian to the required size. If you have difficulty in obtaining 12oz hessian or want to economise, 10oz hessian can be used instead on a small chair.

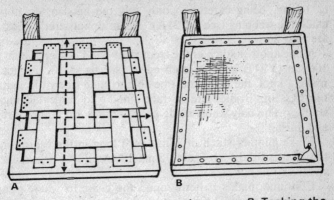

Fig. 30.   *A*: Measure for the hessian cover, *B*: Tacking the hessian.

Place the hessian over the webbing making sure the threads of the hessian run straight from front to back and from side to side.

Turn back the 25mm (1″) turnings upermost and drive in 13mm (½″) tacks approximately 40mm (1½″) apart, through the doubled-back hessian (see fig. 30B). The edge of the hessian should cover the webbing entirely and be tacked to the top of the chair seat rail leaving 13mm (½″) of wood showing all round the edge of the chair.

Make a neat fold at the corners, turning one hem over the other.

BRIDLES

Thread a half-circular needle with enough twine to go one and a half times round the seat of your chair.

Starting in the centre of the right-hand side 75mm-100mm (3″-4″) in from the edge of the seat, make a stitch 25mm

(1") long, being careful to only sew the hessian, do not catch the webbing (see fig. 31A). Tie an upholsterer's knot, see page 26.

Make another stitch at the front right-hand corner 75mm-100mm (3"-4") in from both edges (see fig. 31B). Do not make a knot, the twine must be able to slide freely through the hessian. Bridles are in fact similar to large tacking stitches. The only knots made in the bridles are at the start and finish.

Make another stitch of 25mm (1") long in the centre of the front of the seat, again 75mm-100mm (3"-4") in from the front seat edge.

Continue in this pattern round the chair to where you started, having two bridles across the front, two down each side and one across the back, all being 75mm-100mm (3"-4") in from the outside edge of your chair seat.

Make one bridle across the centre of the seat from side to side and it will now look like fig. 31C.

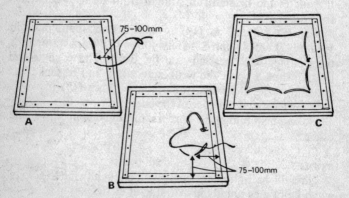

Fig. 31.   A: First stitch for the bridles, B: Second stitch for the bridles, C: The bridles completed.

On small chairs approximately 45cm (14″) or less across the seat front, make four bridles only in the form of a square, 75mm-100mm (3″-4″) in from the outside edge.

If you are working on a large chair seat or sofa seat, then obviously it will be necessary to have extra bridles. Each bridle should be 200mm (8″) or so in length. It would also be necessary to have more than one row of bridles across the centre of the seat. Place both bridles and rows of bridles 200mm (8″) apart.

Do not pull the bridles too tightly. Leave just enough room to be able to slide your hand holding some hair or fibre, underneath each bridle. Then pull a little tighter.

Finish off by tying the twine securely against itself.

FILLING THE BRIDLES

Having washed the hair or bought new stuffing, pick the stuffing over carefully teasing out any lumps.

Do this by holding a small quantity of hair or fibre in your left hand and pulling small strands of hair with your right hand from your left hand. Be sure to tease out all small knots and lumps.

Place small portions of the stuffing in the palm of your hand and push from the middle outwards, partway under the bridles (see fig. 32A). The whispy ends of the stuffing should overhang the edges of the chair by about 25mm (1″).

Start by filling the bridles at the back of your chair seat and work your way round the outside, finally filling the bridles across the centre of your seat.

Do not fold the stuffing in at the edges before putting under the bridles as these bent edges will feel uncomfortable in the seat. Keep the stuffing flat in the palm of your hand with all the ends of the hair or fibre laying flat.

Keep the stuffing evenly distributed and fairly tightly packed.

One can only tell the exact amount of stuffing to go into a chair by experience, but what came out of the chair orig+inally should go back into the chair. As a guide the stuffing

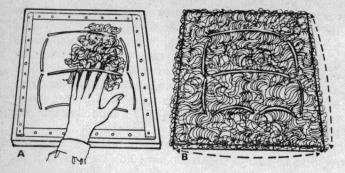

Fig. 32. *A*: The first stuffing, *B*: Measuring for the scrim cover.

should be built up one-third higher than the intended finished first stuffing of your seat, i.e. a seat measuring 75mm (3″) at this stage will compact to 50mm (2″) having been sewn at the end of the first stuffing.

Keep approximately a quarter of your hair or fibre for the second stuffing and for filling the corners of the first stuffing.

When there is enough stuffing in the chair seat, close your eyes and with your fingers curled as for playing the piano, feel for lumps and hollows. Rectify where necessary.

If you have been able to save a small amount of hair only from the original seat of the chair, keep this hair and use it for the second stuffing. Use a cheaper filling such as fibre for the first stuffing.

SCRIM COVER

Measure loosely from one side of the seat rail to the other side of the seat rail at the widest point, over the stuffing and then add 50mm (2″) to this measurement (see fig. 32B). Measure likewise loosely from back to front of the seat rail over the stuffing and add 50mm (2″) to this measurement also.

Cut a piece of scrim or hessian to size. With a pencil mark the centre of each side of the scrim and centre of each seat rail. Place the scrim over the stuffing matching the centre of the scrim edge with the centre of the seat rail (see fig. 33A). Leave a 25mm (1″) turning on the scrim.

Temporarily tack in place with a 13mm (½″) tack the centre of both sides and the centre of the front, matching pencil marks. Do not drive these tacks in fully as they will shortly be taken out again. Do not tack at the back for the moment.

Cut the scrim to go round the chair back struts as follows. Making sure you have enough scrim to reach down to the bottom of the back of the seat rail, fold back the scrim level with the chair back struts.

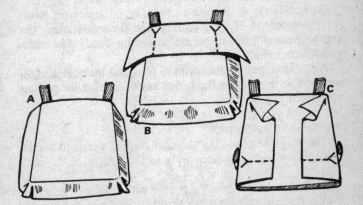

Fig. 33. A: Placing the scrim cover over the hair/stuffing, B: Cutting the scrim to go round the chair back struts, C: Cutting the scrim to go round the chair arms.

Cut the scrim in a line from the outer edge of the scrim down towards the centre of each strut, stopping 25mm (1″) away from the strut (see fig. 33B). Then make a notch, i.e. a small cut to the left at 45° and to the right at 45°, stopping 13mm (½″) away from the strut.

Turn the flap over and tuck down between the chair back struts.

If you have arms to your seat, release the two temporary tacks at either side of the seat rails, fold back the scrim at the sides in line with the arm of the chair. Cut and notch the scrim in the same way as for the back flap, cutting in towards the centre of the arm strut, stopping 25mm (1″) away from the strut and making a "Y" to stop 13mm (½″) away from the upright arm strut (see fig. 33C).

It is now necessary to put in a few temporary tacks so that the scrim will hold the hair in place while you make the "through-stuffing ties". Turn the edges of the scrim in and under. Temporarily tack into the bevelled edge at the top of your seat rail, using 13mm (½″) tacks spaced 175mm (7″) or so apart (see fig. 34A). Temporarily tack at a 45° angle.

Do not worry about the corners, or back or arm struts for the moment. Having worked the through-stuffing ties you will come back to secure the scrim firmly and make good the corners.

Apart from cutting the scrim to go round the back and/or arm struts, do not cut the scrim anywhere else, or cut any corners or edges from it.

THROUGH STUFFING TIES

The reason for making through stuffing ties is to anchor the stuffing firmly and squarely in the centre of the chair seat.

Thread a double pointed needle with a longish length of twine. Push the needle down through the scrim, stuffing and webbing one-third of the way in the from the back edge and one-third of the way in from the left-hand side on a dining room type chair or 150mm (6″) in a larger seat, leaving a

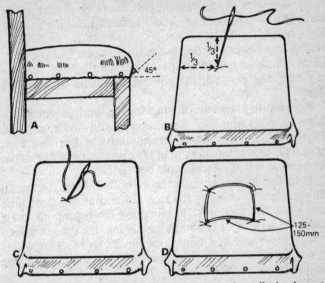

Fig. 34. *A*: Temporarily tack scrim into bevelled edge at top of seat rail, *B*: Through stuffing tie; where to push the needle in, *C*: Bring it up, eye end first, one inch along, *D*: Make four ties, in the form of a square.

length of twine at the top of the seat (see fig. 34B). Move the needle along 25mm (1″) and bring it back up, eye end first, to the top of the seat (see fig. 34C). Tie an upholsterer's knot, see page 26.

There will be four ties each 125mm-150mm (5″-6″) apart in the form of a square in the centre of a dining room type chair seat (see fig. 34D). On a larger chair or sofa seat you will need to make more through stuffing ties, i.e. approximately 125mm-150mm (5″-6″) apart.

Proceed from one tie to the next until you get to the last tie, then put away the needle so as not to damage either the needle or yourself!

Starting with the first stitch, pull the twine at each stitch as tightly as possible ending at the last stitch. Tie the end across at the first knot.

N.B. These ties can be tied individually if you find it easier, in this case tie a half hitch at each of the "ties" before moving onto the next tie. Do not cut the twine between the ties.

Now return to temporarily tacking the scrim in place. The edges of the scrim must be turned in and under, and the 13mm ($\frac{1}{2}$") tacks must be driven into the bevelled edge 50mm (2") apart into the top of the chair seat at a 45° angle. The reason is that they will hold better.

How tightly should the scrim be pulled? Run the thumb of your left hand along the seat rail and at the same time run your left hand first finger along the top of the chair seat; the scrim should now fit loosely into the space between your thumb and first finger (see fig. 35A). In other words the scrim should be just loose enough to take the stitching and thus make a 90° angle.

Temporarily tack to within 25mm (1") of the corners/struts at the back, front and both sides, putting in more stuffing where the edges feel thin.

If necessary, and it probably will be, push extra hair or fibre under the hessian at the front corners and at the back struts.

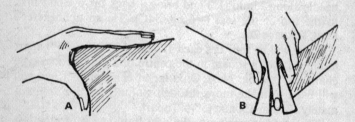

Fig. 35. *A*: Checking the scrim for shape, *B*: Making a square corner.

The corners: Having tacked to within 25mm (1″) of the two front corners, turn the scrim in and under and with one finger at the vertical push the scrim in towards the middle of the seat at 45° angle stopping when level vertically with the chair leg (see fig. 35B). Tack the scrim to the corner with two tacks thus making a 90° angle.

At the back struts, turn in an edge down both sides of each chair leg.

Drive home all tacks when you are satisfied that your seat is a good shape.

Regulate – push the regulator or steel knitting needle through into the scrim and work the hair or fibre to make an even edge all round the chair seat.

If you are upholstering an arm chair or sofa with covered-in arms and back, then stuff the back and sides of your chair seat very firmly. Attach the scrim to the outside of the seat rail. This is because it will not be possible for you to sew the edges of your seat as the covering of the back and arms will prevent it.

THE STITCHED EDGE – BLIND STITCHING

The reason for blind stitching is to anchor the stuffing in that part of the seat that lies between the through stuffing ties, which you have just made, and the rolled edge which you will make.

Before starting to sew, feel the stuffing for any irregularities. Use a regulator, a steel knitting needle or your double-ended needle to even out the irregularities and to work up an even edge where necessary.

With a piece of blackboard or tailor's chalk make a line approximately one-third of the way in between the seat edge and the through stuffing ties. Make a continuous chalk line all round the edge of the chair seat.

Start by stitching along the left-hand side of the seat, followed by the front, then the right-hand side and finally the back. If you are left handed, you may find it more convenient to start on the right-hand side of the seat, followed

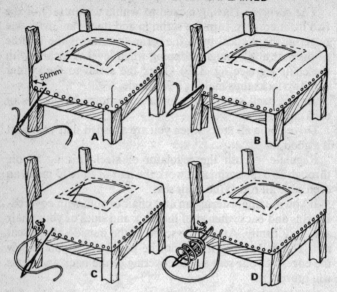

Fig. 36. Stitched edge; blind stitching, *A*: The first stitch, *B*: And back again, *C*: The second stitch, *D*: The knot.

by the front, left-hand side and finally the back. Thread a double-ended needle with 1.20m (4′) of twine. Insert the needle 50mm (2″) forward from the left-hand back strut at a point just above the tacks (see fig. 36A). Push the needle upwards and partially out of the scrim emerging at the chalk line. Do not pull the needle completely out of the scrim, bring it out only as far as the eye of the needle. Stop, reverse the direction and bring the needle out 25mm (1″) away from the strut at the back of the chair seat, just above the tack line (see fig. 36B).

Tie an upholsterer's knot (see page 26). Pull the twine tight.

Put on a glove. The twine when being pulled tightly is apt to hurt one's hand. An old leather or gardening glove will overcome this. However, remember you can now pull more forcefully so be careful not to overpull and break the twine.

Now carry on, repeating the italicised instructions below over and over again, until you reach the corner.

Insert the needle into the scrim 50mm (2") further along, come out as far as the eye of the needle at the chalk line (see fig. 36C). Stop, reverse direction and bring the needle partway out 25mm (1") back from where you went in. It will be the "eye" end of the needle that will emerge.

Take hold of the twine coming out of the scrim on your left, and twist it round the end of the needle that is pointing out of the scrim three times (see fig. 36D).

Pull the needle out and pull the knot tight, pulling first to the left and then to the right.

To sew round a corner or the chair strut, sew to within 25mm (1") of the corner, insert the needle into the scrim, come out into the top of the seat 50mm (2") in from the seat edge, stop, twist the needle by 90° and come straight out at the other side of the corner or strut. Do not twist the twine round the needle on this occasion. Proceed as before.

Keep the line of stitching on the edge of the chair seat to a line just above the tacks. Be sure to keep your stitching line straight and low. You will spoil the finished effect if you allow your stitching line to wander or rise up the edge of your chair seat.

You will begin to notice the stuffing between the centre ties and the seat edge is beginning to flatten. This is because the twine is holding the stuffing very tightly. You will also notice that the scrim and stuffing edge is beginning to hang over the edge of the chair frame. Don't worry, you are doing all right – it is just as it should be.

If your chair has a deep seat it will be necessary to work a second row of blind stitching above the first row. If you are unsure as to whether or not to work a second row, carry on and work the rolled edge and if the distance between the two rows of stitching is greater than 30mm (1¼″) then work a second row of blind stitching above the first row, emerging the needle between where the needle came out on the first row and the inside of the rolled edge.

If your arm chair or sofa has padded arms and back then you will be able to work a row of blind stitching along the front edge only.

If you have a padded back but no arms, then work the blind stitching round the front and both sides.

ROLLED EDGE

The reason for the rolled edge is to make a good firm edge, which will stand up to many years' of constant battering. It is most important to make a good job of stitching your rolled edge. Keep the edge evenly stuffed, standing upright and level with the edge of the chair frame.

Before starting to sew, examine the stuffing again for any irregularities and work up the stuffing to an even edge with your regulator, where necessary.

With your piece of chalk make another line, this time 25mm (1″) in from the rounded edge of the scrim, all round the edge of the seat.

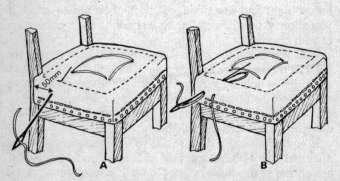

Fig. 37. *A*: Rolled edge: the first stitch, *B*: And back again.

Thread a needle with 1.20m (4') of twine.

Starting in the same place and working in the same direction as for the blind stitching, insert the needle 50mm (2'') forward from the left-hand back strut and 13mm ($\frac{1}{2}$'') above the line of the blind stitching (see fig. 37A). This time pull the needle out of the scrim on top of the seat at the new chalk line, but do not pull the twine right through.

Move backwards towards the chair back strut for 25mm (1'') and push the eye of the needle back downwards through the scrim (see fig. 37B). Tie an upholsterer's knot, see page 26. Pull the twine tight.

Now carry on, repeating the italicised instructions below over and over again, until you reach the corner.

Move forward 50mm (2'') towards the front of the chair, insert the needle into the scrim 13mm ($\frac{1}{2}$'') above the last stitching line and bring the needle out at the chalk line. Do not pull all the twine right through the scrim (see fig. 38A).

Move backwards for 25mm (1'') towards the chair back, insert the eye end of the needle into the scrim at the chalk line and pull the needle halfway through emerging 13mm ($\frac{1}{2}$'') above the last stitching line.

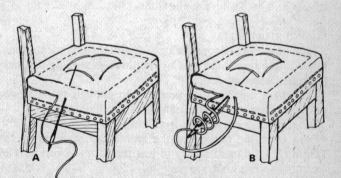

Fig. 38. *A*: The second stitch, *B*: The knot.

Take hold of the twine coming out of the scrim on your left and twist it round the end of the needle that is pointing out of the scrim, three times (see fig. 38B).

Pull the needle out and pull the knot tightly, first to the left and then to the right, and at the same time take the roll in your left hand and gently squeeze the roll into an upright position. The roll should make a hard straight edge to your seat and should make a continuation in a straight line of the chair seat rail.

If your chair seat has a deep seat the distance between the blind stitching and the rolled edge stitching will be more than 13mm ($\frac{1}{2}$″).

Work a blind stitch round the corner as before, i.e. work to within 25mm (1″) of the corner, push the needle in emerging 25mm (1″) into the seat, as far as the eye of the needle, turn and come out at the other side of the corner.

Continue to work a roll round all four sides of the chair, working a blind stitch at each corner and round the chair back strut.

If your chair or sofa has padded arms and back then you will be able to make a rolled edge across the seat front only. A seat with a padded back but no arms will have a rolled edge round both sides and the front.

SECOND STUFFING

The object of a second stuffing is to fill up the indentations made in the top of the seat by the through stuffing ties and the rolled edge.

Thread a half circular needle with enough twine to go once completely round the outside of the chair seat.

Starting in the left-hand front corner 75mm-100mm (3″-4″) in from the outside of the front edge, make a stitch 25mm (1″) long and taking in just the scrim covering. Tie an upholsterer's knot, see page 26.

Make long tacking stitches, one in each of the four corners of the seat, 75mm-100mm (3″-4″) in from the edge. Tie a knot to secure the twine against the upholsterer's knot at the start, thus making four bridles (see fig. 39A).

On larger seats, two bridles will be needed across the front and on both sides, and across the middle of the seat. Sofa seats will need bridles approximately 200mm (8″) long with 200mm (8″) between rows of bridles.

Place a small amount of stuffing under each bridle. The amount of stuffing used for this second stuffing will be a little less than a quarter of that used for the first stuffing (see fig. 39B).

WADDING

The reason for putting wadding on top of the second stuffing is to stop the small fibres working their way through to the top cover and feeling prickly. It also helps to make a more comfortable seat.

Measure from the lower sewing line on one side of the chair seat to the lower sewing line on the other side of the chair seat at the widest point. Measure likewise from the lower sewing line at the back of the chair seat to the lower sewing line at the front of the chair seat.

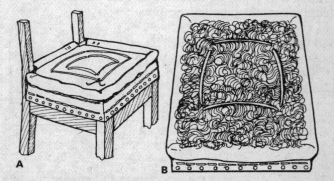

Fig. 39. *A*: Four bridles for the second stuffing, *B*: Second stuffing completed.

Tear a piece of cotton wadding or similar to size. Cotton wadding can be "pulled" apart rather than being cut with scissors, this will make a softer edge.

If your seat has a large expanse of wooden seat rail to be covered, measure to within 25mm (1″) of the bottom of the seat rail.

For a chair or sofa seat with a padded back and arms allow enough wadding to fit well down under the back and arms.

Place the wadding carefully and centrally on top of the chair seat to cover the second stuffing and to hang partway down over the edge of the seat.

Tear the wadding in the two places opposite the two back struts, leaving the flap between the two tears to fit nicely down between the two back struts (see fig. 40A). Do likewise at the arm struts if appropriate.

Tear off the excess pieces of wadding on the outside edge of the back tear, so that the edge of the wadding will lay flush vertically against the chair's back leg.

Fig. 40. *A*: Tearing the wadding to fit between the two back struts, *B*: Take out a square of wadding at the front corners.

Take out a square of wadding at both front corners, so that the wadding will meet at the corner and not overlap (see fig. 40B).

CALICO COVER

The reason for having a calico cover under the top cover is threefold: first you can pull the calico really tight and make a good seat shape on a cover, without its showing if it gets a bit grubby in the process. Secondly, it makes a good trial run before putting on your top cover and if you do make a mistake with the cutting it is not so disastrous as making a mistake on an expensive piece of material. Thirdly, if at a later date you want to change the top cover of your chair, having a calico cover underneath will make the operation very much easier.

While it is not essential to have a calico cover therefore, it is to be recommended.

Measure from the bottom edge of one side seat rail to the bottom edge of the other side seat rail at the widest point; add 50mm (2″) for holding. Measure likewise from the bottom edge of the front seat rail to the bottom edge of the back seat rail, add 50mm (2″) for holding.

Cut a piece of calico, curtain lining, sheeting or a similar new strongly woven fabric to size.

ATTACHING THE CALICO

With a pencil, mark the centre of the back of the calico and the centre of the back of the seat rail. Do likewise at the centre of the front and both sides. Place the calico over the wadding, matching the pencil lines and allowing the excess calico to fall evenly round the chair seat. Don't put in any tacks for the moment.

Cut the calico to go round the chair back strut as follows. Making sure you have enough calico to reach down to the bottom of the back of the seat rail, fold back the calico level with the chair back struts.

Cut the calico in a line from the outer edge of the calico

down towards the centre of each strut, stopping 25mm (1")
away from the strut. Then make a notch (i.e. a small cut to
the left at 45° and to the right at 45° and thus making a
"Y" shape cut in the material) stopping 13mm ($\frac{1}{2}$") away
from the strut.

Turn the flap over and tuck down between the chair back
struts. By pulling the calico at each side of the chair back
strut, the "Y" will slide down between the seat and the
strut, thus making a nice neat corner. Do not cut the fabric
at the arm struts just yet.

Turn the edge in and under and temporarily tack the
back only with 13mm ($\frac{1}{2}$") tacks, turning in the calico vertically by the back struts. The tacks should be spaced 40mm
(1$\frac{1}{2}$") apart (see fig. 41A).

If your chair has show wood, keep the tacks high above
the show wood, so as to leave room for the tacks holding
the top cover to go between the tacks holding the calico and
the show wood. (Show wood is the polished wood that shows
round the bottom of the seat on all sides of the chair.)

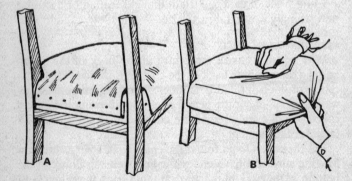

Fig. 41.   A: Temporarily tack the calico to the back, B: Pull
the calico forward tightly.

If your chair has no show wood, temporarily tack the calico 25mm (1″) from the bottom of the seat rail.

Pull the calico forward to the front of the seat. The calico must be pulled forward as tightly as possible. This is probably best done by running the knuckle of your right-hand thumb across the seat from back to front and at the same time pulling the calico forward with your left hand (see fig. 41B). It is not necessary to turn under a hem when attaching calico, indeed it is very much easier not to. However it does help to give strength when pulling if the calico at the back of the chair has been attached double.

Keeping the tack line in a similar place as at the back of the chair, push a 13mm ($\frac{1}{2}$″) tack in as far as you can by hand (thank heavens for those long sharp points), balancing it on top of your thumb nail while you reach for your hammer. This is one of those times when you could well do with a third hand!

N.B. Remember to drive the tacks in partway only. When you have secured the calico in more places along the chair front, the calico at the first tacks can generally be pulled tighter.

Pull down the calico in the same way along the front of the chair seat stopping 100mm (4″) short of each corner at the front only.

Keeping the tack line in a similar position to the front and back, temporarily tack both sides of the seat, starting in the centre and working outwards. Stop 25mm (1″) back from the front corner.

Cut the spare calico off towards the back of each side by the chair leg, leaving enough for a turning. Turn under the vertical edge by the chair's back leg, and pulling down tightly, temporarily tack to hold in place.

Front corners (assuming you have square 90° corners on your chair). If you haven't already, tack up to 25mm (1″) of the corner on one side, pull the calico hard round the corner horizontally and then very slightly downwards. Drive in a tack fully (see fig. 42A).

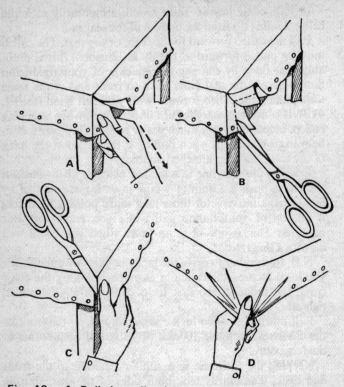

Fig. 42. *A*: Pull the calico hard round the corner, *B*: Cut away excess calico from inside of corner, *C*: Making a neat square corner, *D*: Pulling the calico down for a rounded front corner.

Fold the calico to make a straight line vertically exactly at the corner Run the calico between your finger and thumb so as to make a permanent crease. Cut a line upwards 25mm (1″) away from the tack at the corner, turn at a 90° angle and cut back down the calico 40mm (1½″) inside from the crease (see fig. 42B).

Fold the calico under at the crease and hold in position at the corner. Run the flat end of a regulator or the points of your closed scissors up the crease between the two pieces of calico, at the same time pulling the calico downwards very tightly (see fig. 42C). Tack in position. Repeat for the other corner.

Drive in all temporary tacks when you are satisfied that the calico has been pulled as tight as possible and you can make no wrinkles in it. It is very important that this operation is done as well as possible.

You can probably get away with not sewing the calico at the fold on the corners, but you must sew the fold on the top cover. However if the calico looks a bit untidy at the corners, it would be as well to sew a neat seam.

If your "square" corner has a rounded look, gently tap the calico and wadding with a mallet to make a better shape.

If your chair has rounded front corners; take hold of the calico in the centre of the corner and pull down hard. Temporarily tack (see fig. 42D). You will now have a surplus of calico on both sides of the centre tack. This surplus needs to be folded into one or two small pleats on either side of the centre tack to form a "fan" appearance.

TOP COVER

If you have not already bought your top cover fabric, now is the time to measure for it and buy it. Remember to add on a little extra for holding.

Putting on your top cover fabric will now be easy because you have done all the hard work getting a good finish to your chair seat at the calico stage.

You will also have learnt by exeprience with the calico exactly how to do it.

If your seat rail is narrow and your top fabric is not too thick, 10mm ($\frac{3}{8}''$) tacks can be used instead of 13mm ($\frac{1}{2}''$) tacks.

If you are working on a hall sofa or small armchair, now

is the time to take off the old top cover, add a layer of wadding and recover with new fabric. Make a note of how you take off the old cover and put the new fabric on in exactly the same way. However the outside back and outside arms must wait until the seat as well as the back and inside arms have been recovered.

If you have show wood round the base of your chair seat, measure from the show wood at the back of the chair, over the seat and down to the show wood at the front of the chair seat. Add 25mm (1″) extra for holding the fabric. Measure likewise from the show wood on one side of the chair seat to the show wood on the other side. Add 25mm (1″) extra for holding the fabric. Cut a piece of your top cover fabric to this size, centring the pattern.

If you have no show wood on your chair and you do not want to have braid, then measure 25mm (1″) under the back seat rail, up the back of the seat, across the top of the seat, down the front of the seat and 25mm (1″) under the front seat rail. Add 25mm (1″) extra for holding the fabric.

Measure likewise across the seat to get the width measurement. Cut a piece of your top cover fabric to this size, centering the pattern.

This piece of top cover fabric is attached to the chair in exactly the same way as the calico. The top cover must be pulled tightly over the seat, but it won't be such a battle as it was with the calico. Remember to centre the pattern, if any.

Using a half circular needle and ladder stitch, sew the corners with a matching button thread.

To work ladder stitch :— Make a small stitch into and out of the edge of the fabric on the right of the two pieces of fabric to be joined. Where the needle emerges, go straight across to the other piece of fabric on the left of the join (see fig. 43A).

Make a similar stitch going in and out of that piece of fabric (see fig. 43B). Where the thread crosses over between

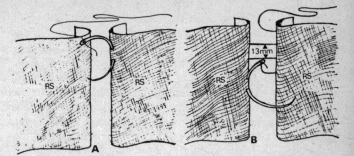

Fig. 43. Ladder stitch, *A*: First small stitch on the right, *B*: Across to the left and back. Pull cotton to make stitches invisible.

one piece of fabric and the other is similar to a rung of a ladder, hence its name: ladder stitch. Pull tight as you go.

To attach the braid, put a thin film of clear Bostik or Uhu onto the back of the braid and press down onto the fabric to cover the tack heads. Make a neat fold at each corner. Cover the first end of the braid by placing the folded other end on top.

Drive in a matching coloured gimp pin at each corner and two others spaced evenly on each side.

If you cannot buy gimp pins to match, they can easily be coloured by either painting with a paintbrush or putting into a small pot of enamel paint. Care must be taken when hammering not to chip off the enamel.

BLACK CLOTH – DUST COVER

Finally the underside of the seat needs to be covered for neatness and to keep in the dust (see fig. 44A).

This is generally done with a piece of upholsterer's black cloth, but can just as easily be done with a piece of left over

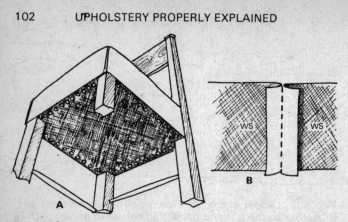

Fig. 44. *A*: Cover underside to finish, *B*: Seam together two left over pieces of hessian.

hessian or scrim. You can join together with a neat seam on the sewing machine two pieces of hessian to form a piece large enough to cover the underside of the chair seat (see fig. 44B).

Turn under 25mm (1″) turnings and attach with 13mm (½″) tacks, 50mm (2″) apart.

For posterity and the amusement of future generations, attach to the inside of the seat rail a note of your name, the date, and the cost of materials used. Probably in fifty years time the exorbitant cost of your materials will seem ludicrously cheap!

5

SPRUNG SEAT
(TRADITIONAL UPHOLSTERY)

SHOPPING LIST

... m/yds webbing

... springs

... m/yds spring hessian

... lbs stuffing

... m/yds scrim

16mm ($\frac{5}{8}''$) tacks

13mm ($\frac{1}{2}''$) tacks

10mm ($\frac{3}{8}''$) tacks

... m/yds cotton wadding

... m/yds calico

... m/yds top cover fabric

... m/yds braid

laid cord

twine

adhesive

Black cloth – optional

It is being assumed that it is the seat only of your chair or sofa that will need to be reupholstered. It is quite probable that the back and/or arms will only need recovering with a little padding added. Therefore allow cotton wadding and calico for the inside of the back and arms only, but measure both inside back and outside back – also inside and outside arms if appropriate – as well as the seat when calculating the amount of top cover fabric needed. The braid measurements also will need adjusting. (See chapter 7 – top cover for your wing-backed chair).

Take your measurements for your shopping list before you start to strip your chair if you wish.

Turn your chair upside down. If it has black cloth or similar tacked to the bottom, remove it so that you can then see the webbing attached to the chair frame and the springs up above the webbing.

WEBBING: 50mm (2") wide black and white webbing is ideal. Measure that part of each length of webbing that you can actually see and add 100mm (4") for turnunders, i.e.; 25mm (1") at each end which is hidden from view and 25mm (1") for turnunders. Add up the measurements of the webbing and add 250mm-300mm (10"-12") so that you will be able to have enough webbing for tensioning on the final web.

The strands of webbing should not be more than 50mm (2") apart. If on your chair they are, measure for extra strands of webbing as appropriate.

SPRINGS: In your chair you may be able to see any number of springs from a solitary single spring upwards. For a dining room chair buy four 5" springs (or four 6" springs if you want a deeper seat). Arm chairs generally have nine or twelve 6" or 7" whereas sofas and big armchairs will have more and deeper springs.

LAID CORD: Some upholsterers will sell small hanks of laid cord, sufficient for one chair. The cord used for tying down the springs must be very strong if you cannot buy upholsterers' laid cord.

SPRING HESSIAN: Measure over the top of the chair seat if it is still upholstered, from side to side including both outside edges and add 50mm (2") for turnings. Measure over the top from the back to the front of the seat including the back outside edge and the front outside edge and add 50mm (2") for turnings.

12oz spring hessian is stronger than 10oz and is more suitable when covering springs.

STUFFING: If there is horse hair in your chair seat, wash and reuse it. Otherwise buy 2 lbs of hair, black fibre or curly coir for a dining room chair, or 3 lbs if you have a larger seat. Armchair seats can take as much as 6-8 lbs and sofas proportionately more.

SCRIM: Measure as for the hessian but the final measurements of both the length measurement and the width measurement should be 100mm (4″) larger than that of the hessian.

Scrim is easier to work but if you can't find it in your shop then use a 10oz hessian.

COTTON WADDING: Measure as for the spring hessian, but do not add on the turning allowances because the wadding does not have to be turned under round the edges.

Remember to measure for the inside of your back and/or arms if appropriate.

CALICO: Measure as for the spring hessian, remembering to add on the 50mm (2″) turnunders. Also remember to measure for the inside of your back and/or arms if appropriate.

TOP COVER FABRIC: The measurements for the top cover will be the same as for the calico, except if there is a pattern on the chosen fabric you must allow for centering the pattern. However it is often sensible to complete the job of reupholstering your chair before buying the fabric for the top cover.

BRAID: If there is braid on your chair already, measure all the braid and allow a little extra for corners etc.

If there is no braid on your chair and there should be, then measure all the way round the chair seat, add a little extra for corners and turnings.

Sometimes there will be no show wood on the chair seat and the top cover fabric will be taken right down the sides of the chair and fastened underneath the chair, in which case there is no need for braid. The only reason for having braid is to cover the tack heads.

Sofas and armchairs generally do not have braid on them.
BLACK CLOTH: Measure underneath the chair seat and add
50mm (2") to both the length and the width measurements
for turnunders. The reason for the black cloth is that it
acts as a dust cover. Not all chairs have black cloth and you
can just as easily use some pieces of left-over hessian. You
can even sew two pieces of hessian together to make one
piece that is big enough to fit under your chair.

TACKS: 4oz of 16mm ($\frac{5}{8}$") Improved and 6oz of 13mm ($\frac{1}{2}$")
fine Upholsterer's tacks, not bayonet tacks. However if the
wood on top of your frame is only 25mm (1") or so wide,
it would be safer and less likely to split the wood if you
were to use 13mm ($\frac{1}{2}$") tacks instead of the 16mm ($\frac{5}{8}$") tacks
for the webbing. Likewise drop down one size and use
10mm ($\frac{3}{8}$") instead of 13mm ($\frac{1}{2}$") tacks for the hessian and
calico etc.

For large armchairs and sofas buy double quantity of
tacks.

TWINE: As upholsterer's comes in rather a big and expensive ball, try to persuade an upholsterer to sell you a small
quantity, some sell small hanks of approximately 20 yards.
It is well worth while to buy the real thing; for a start it is
so much easier to work with and for another it is stronger.

Having done your shopping and bought the necessary
materials, gather up your tools needed for the next job
which is "stripping and preparing the frame" see page
20.

If you are upholstering a sofa or arm chair, leave the
existing top cover on the inside back and arms so as to
keep the present upholstery undisturbed until you are ready
to put on the new top cover fabric.

WEBBING

16mm ($\frac{5}{8}$") improved tacks should be used for attaching
2" wide black and white webbing to the seat.

Because your chair is to have springs in it the webbing should be attached to the underneath of the seat rail. So, turn your chair upside down.

In the case of a dining room type chair, turn it upside down and lay the seat onto the seat of another similar sized chair. See fig. 45A. To prevent damage to the show wood on the back of the chair, place an old cushion or rug on the floor under the top bar of the back of the chair.

Take care to space the strands of webbing evenly across the seat, and the space between each piece of webbing should not be wider than the width of the webbing, i.e.; in this case 50mm (2").

Measure the length of the bottom of the front seat rail, divide the inches by two to get the number of webs and spaces that will fit onto the seat rail (see fig. 45B). If you have an uneven number you will either have to have more spaces than webs or vice versa.

Try to make the new webbing come at a place where there are no holes from the tacks holding the previous webbing in place.

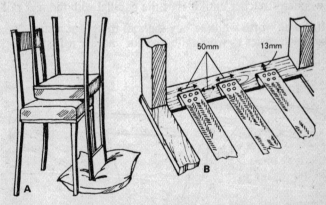

Fig. 45.   A: Method of turning chair upside down and laying seat onto seat of a similar-sized chair, B: Spacing the webbing.

With a pencil, mark on the underside of the seat rail the places where the webbing will come.

Measure, divide and mark the places on the underside of the back rail where the webbing is to come. Very often the back of a chair is narrower than the front of a chair and therefore the strands of webbing will be slightly closer together at the back of the chair.

Measure, divide and mark the places on the undersides of both sides of the chair where the webbing is to come.

Take your piece of webbing, turn under 25mm (1″) and place the webbing 13mm (½″) back in from the outside edge of the bottom of the seat rail. Secure with five 16mm (⅝″) tacks (see fig. 46A).

You must attach the webbing to the other side of the frame under tension. Use a web stretcher or wind the webbing over the top of your piece of wood, back underneath and up to cover the end nearest the seat rail, with the webbing pulled fairly taut over the wood and the wood at a slight upward angle (see fig. 46B).

Tighten the webbing by pressing downwards on the wooden stretcher until it is at the parallel with the seat rail.

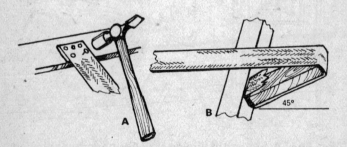

Fig. 46. *A*: Attaching the first end, *B*: Tensioning the webbing at the other end.

Put in three 16mm ($\frac{5}{8}''$) tacks in a straight line, one at each corner and one in the middle, 13mm ($\frac{1}{2}''$) in from the outside edge of the seat rail.

Cut the webbing, leaving 50mm (2") clear from the tacks. Turn the webbing over and drive in two more 16mm ($\frac{5}{8}''$) tacks in a position between the three tacks already holding the webbing and slightly forward of them (see fig. 47A).

Complete all the webbing in one direction first before starting to web in the other direction. When webbing in the other direction, the webbing must be interlaced as when weaving (see fig. 47B).

Turn the chair back into an upright position.

SPRINGS

Use 5" springs on a dining room type chair, unless you want a deep seat, in which case use 6" springs. Arm chairs and sofas will of course need more and bigger springs.

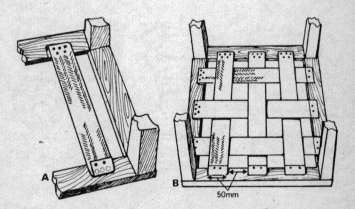

Fig. 47. A: Drive in the last two tacks, B: Webbing must be interlaced.

Stand the springs in an upright position on the webbing trying to get them centred with as much webbing underneath each spring as possible. Either stand them where the strands of webbing cross each other (fig. 48A) or so the entire bottom coil of the spring is sitting on webbing (fig. 48B).

Although it is not necessary, you will find it very much easier when lashing the springs, if they are all in straight vertical and horizontal lines, therefore four springs in two rows is preferable to five springs with the extra one in the middle of the four. (On larger seats have six springs in two rows or nine springs in three rows etc.)

Also, not necessary but easier when it comes to lashing the springs, make all the knots on the top of the springs face the same way, i.e.; at ten minutes to the hour or north north west (see fig. 48C).

The springs should be centred and equidistant from each other. Don't put the springs too near to the outside seat rails.

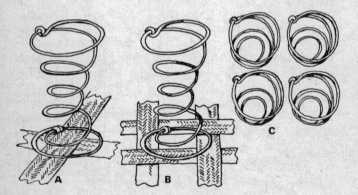

Fig. 48. *A*: Stand the springs where the webs cross, *B*: Or so that the entire bottom coil is sitting on webbing, *C*: And with all the top spring knots facing 10 o'clock.

SEWING THE SPRINGS

Each spring must be secured in four places with twine and a knot.

Remove for the moment the front row of springs and start by attaching the springs at the back of the chair. Take a longish piece of upholsterer's twine and thread your long double ended needle (or mattress needle if you have got one, which is slightly shorter but still with a big eye and a strong body).

Starting at the spring at the right hand back corner, push the needle down through the webbing as close to the outside edge of the bottom coil of the spring as possible. Bring the needle back up on the inside of the same spring and tie an upholsterer's knot, see page 26. Then follow the italicised instructions below, repeating for each quarter of each spring.

Push the needle down close to the same coil again and close to (the knot on) the outside of the coil, leaving a loop of twine on the top of the chair (see fig. 49A). Return the needle close to the coil on the inside (see fig. 49B).

Before pulling the needle right through take hold of the end of the loop furthest away from the needle, (i.e.; one end of the loop will give if you pull it and the other end won't – take hold of the end that won't pull). Wind the twine round the point of the needle 8 times, keeping the first twist pulled fairly tightly (see fig. 49C).

Pull the needle up through this "French knot" with one hand while holding the knot between the fingers of the other hand. If you find it hard to pull the needle through the knot, slightly loosen the knot.

Pull the needle back down on the outside of the coil (see fig. 49D).

Pull the twine tightly so that the "French knot" makes a "bridge" over the coil of the spring (see fig. 49E). This bridge will hold the spring firmly in position over many years and much wear.

Run the twine along underneath the webbing to the next quarter of the same spring and repeat this italicised section.

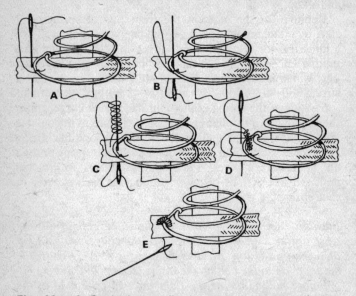

Fig. 49. *A*: Push the needle down through the webbing outside the spring leaving a loop on the top, *B*: Return the needle close to the coil on the inside, *C*: Before pulling it right through, wind the twine round the point of the needle eight times, *D*: Pull the needle through and push it back down on the outside of the coil, *E*: The finished bridge.

When the length of twine has been used up, finish the existing bridge, then tie the twine tightly round a piece of twine running between two bridges on the underside of the webbing. Start the new piece of twine as before with an upholsterer's knot.

Make four bridges evenly over each spring, running the twine along underneath the webbing from bridge to bridge and from spring to spring.

When you have sewn in all the springs in the back row, return the springs to the chair for the front row. Position in line.

LASHING THE SPRINGS

The reason for lashing the springs is to keep them in an upright position. A chair seat will become uncomfortable if the laid cord holding the springs breaks.

Measuring over the top of a row of springs, measure and cut a length of laid cord twice the length of the seat to tie down the springs in that row (see fig. 50A).

Tie a knot some distance back in from the end of the laid cord. The distance from the knot to the end of the twine should be long enough to reach from the rail of the chair to the top coil of the nearest spring and sufficient for three knots.

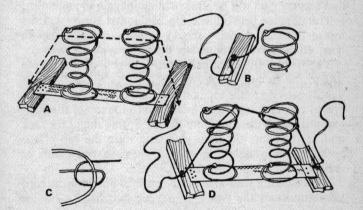

Fig. 50.   *A*: Measure over the top of the springs and double the length, *B*: Hammer in a 16mm tack, *C*: A half-hitch, *D*: Showing the half hitches on the springs.

Into the centre of this knot, place a 16mm ($\frac{5}{8}''$) improved tack (see fig. 50B). Hammer this tack into the top of the seat rail in line with the centre of the row of springs.

Take hold of the longer end of the laid cord and while depressing the spring with your hand to two thirds of its normal size, tie a half-hitch to the second coil down of the first spring. Then tie a half hitch onto the top coil at the opposite side of the same spring.

To make a half hitch: Take the cord over the top of the coil of the spring to be lashed, turn and come back underneath the coil, up over the top of the laid cord, down beside the cord, under the spring and continue on to the next spring (see fig. 50C).

Having secured the first spring with two half hitches, carry on to the second spring. Tie a half hitch to the top coil of the second spring at the side nearest to the first spring.

Having taken your hand away from the top of the first spring it will be leaning over in rather a drunken fashion, don't worry, you will be straightening it again in a moment.

The distance between the top of the first spring and the top of the second spring should be the same as the space between them at their bases (see fig. 51A).

The first and the last half hitch in a row of springs are tied to the second coil down, whereas the rest of the half hitches are tied to the top coil (see fig. 50D).

Drive a 16mm ($\frac{5}{8}''$) tack halfway into the top of the front seat rail. Wind the cord from the last spring round the tack and at the same time lay your arm over the top of the springs already lashed to depress them to two/thirds of their original height (see fig. 51B).

Before taking your arm off the springs but with the cord taking most of the strain, with your free hand wind the cord once more round the tack head and hammer the tack home fully.

If the row of springs on your chair or sofa is longer than your arm, use a strong wooden board.

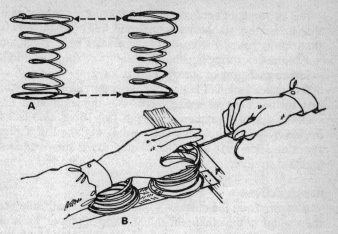

Fig. 51. *A*: Distance between tops of springs should be same as at bases, *B*: Lay arm over top of springs already lashed to depress them.

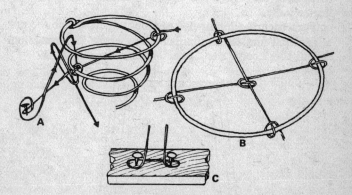

Fig. 52. *A*: The first of the last three half-hitches, *B*: Twist cords together where they cross, *C*: Two tacks for extra strength on large seats.

The two ends of cord can now be taken over the top coil of their nearest respective springs and tied with three half hitch knots round the cord that originally went from the tack to the first spring (see fig. 52A).

Secure each row of springs in this way.

Where one length of laid cord crosses over another length, twist the two together (see fig. 52B).

On sofa and large chair seats, put two 16mm ($\frac{5}{8}$″) tacks in side by side to hold the laid cord at each end of a row of springs. The cord should be twisted round the two tacks for extra strength (see fig. 52C).

HESSIAN COVER

Measure from the outside of one side of the seat rail over the springs to the other seat rail and add 50mm (2″) to this measurement. Measure likewise from the outside of the back seat rail, over the springs, to the outside of the front seat rail and add 50mm (2″) to this measurement also.

Cut a piece of spring hessian to the required size.

Place the hessian over the springs, making sure the threads of the weave run straight from front to back and horizontally.

Turn back the 25mm (1″) turnings uppermost so the raw edges show until the stuffing is put on (see fig. 53). Use 13mm

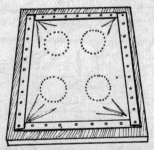

Fig. 53.   Attaching the hessian, turnings uppermost.

($\frac{1}{2}''$) tacks to secure the doubled-back hessian to the seat rail. Put the tacks approximately 40mm ($1\frac{1}{2}''$) apart.

Make a neat fold at the corners.

STITCHING THE SPRINGS

To secure the spring to the hessian use a needle and twine. Because the springs are such an important part of the chair and take so much punishment over the years, they need to be secured in three places to make sure of their staying firmly where they are meant to. You have already sewn them to the webbing, lashed them to the seat rails of the chair and now you are going to sew them once again to the spring hessian, but this time it is very quick and easy!

Thread a half circular needle with a longish length of twine and starting with the back right hand spring push the needle down through the hessian on one side and close to the spring. Bring it back up again close to and on the other side of the spring. Do not catch anything in the twine except the hessian and the coil of the spring (i.e. no webbing or laid cord) (see fig. 54A). Tie an upholsterer's knot, see page 26.

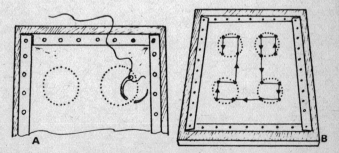

Fig. 54. *A*: First stitch (upholsterer's knot) on the springs, *B*: Pattern of the remaining stitches (single knots).

Each spring must be tied in four places, so move along on the top of the hessian to the next quarter and tie a single knot. Carry on, following the pattern shown in fig. 54B.

Do not cut the twine between the knots and always run along from knot to knot on the top of the hessian. Keep the twine taut.

When the first piece of twine has been used up, tie a knot against one of the lengths of twine running between two knots. Start again with a fresh piece of twine and an upholsterer's knot.

Having completed the sewing of the springs, the remainder of a sprung seat is worked in the same way as an unsprung seat. Therefore please turn to page 79 and follow the instructions starting with the bridles. Work through the sections to the final top cover in the same way as for an unsprung seat.

6

CHAIR SEAT
UPHOLSTERED WITH FOAM

SHOPPING LIST

... m/yds Pirelli webbing
... x ... 2" thick foam
... x ... 1" thick foam
16mm improved tacks
13mm tacks
Adhesive for foam

... m/yds terylene wadding
... m/yds calico
... m/yds top cover fabric
... m/yds braid – optional
... m/yds black cloth, optional
Adhesive for braid

You can take the measurements for your shopping list before you start to strip your chair.

Turn your chair upside down. If it has black cloth or another fabric tacked to the bottom you may find it easier to remove it, so that you can see the webbing.

WEBBING: Measure the length of each of the strands of webbing; add 50mm (2") to each strand for that part that is hidden from view. Measure the webbing in both directions.

If you are using 50mm (2″) wide Pirelli webbing, see that the strands of webbing are 50mm (2″) apart and no more.

Add up the measurements of the strands of webbing, counting both horizontal and vertical strands. Add 200mm-300mm (8″-10″) for the tensioning on the last strand.

FOAM – *50mm (2″) thick:* Make a paper template 6mm ($\frac{1}{4}$″) larger all round than the frame of your chair seat. Take this template shopping with you; hopefully the shopkeeper may well cut you a piece of 50mm (2″) thick foam to the size and shape of your template.

FOAM – *25mm (1″) thick:* Have the shopkeeper also cut you a piece of 25mm (1″) thick foam 50mm (2″) smaller all round than the large piece of foam.

CALICO: You will need a piece of calico 75mm (3″) larger all round, i.e. on all four sides, than the largest piece of foam, i.e. the 50mm (2″) thick piece. You will also need four strips of calico, 100mm (4″) deep by the length of each of the measurements between the legs of the chair.

TERYLENE WADDING: The measurements for the terylene wadding will be the same as for the 50mm (2″) thick foam, plus 100mm (4″).

TOP COVER: The measurements for the top cover fabric will be the same as those for the terylene wadding, but add an extra 100mm (4″) to each measurement if the top cover fabric is to go down and round to the underside of the chair seat. Add 50mm (2″) extra if the top cover fabric is to go down as far as the show wood only.

BRAID: Measure all round the chair seat, add 50mm (2″) extra for corners and turnings. It is not necessary to have braid if your top cover fabric is being attached to the underside of the chair seat.

BLACK CLOTH: Measure underneath the chair seat and add 50mm (2″) to both the length and width measurements for turnunders. The reason for the black cloth is that it acts as a dust cover. Not all chairs have black cloth and you can just as easily use some left over pieces of calico. These can be sewn together to give one large piece if necessary and thus be big enough to fit under your chair.

TACKS: 4oz of 16mm improved and 4oz of 13mm Upholsterer's tacks, not bayonet tacks. However if the wood on the top of your frame is only 25mm (1″) or so wide, it would be safer and less likely to split the wood if you were to use 13mm ($\frac{1}{2}$″) tacks instead of 16mm ($\frac{5}{8}$″) tacks for the webbing. Likewise drop down one size and use 10mm ($\frac{3}{8}$″) instead of 13mm ($\frac{1}{2}$″) tacks for the calico and top cover.

Having bought the materials on your shopping list, gather up your tools and start by stripping your chair of all the old upholstery.

Pirelli webbing takes the place of both the webbing and the springs used in traditional upholstery.

Use 50mm (2″) wide Pirelli webbing for chair seats. Narrower webbing can be used on the arms and back.

The strands of webbing should be spaced evenly over the seat, and the space between each piece of webbing should not be wider than the width of the webbing to be used.

Measure the length of the top of the front seat rail, divide the inches by two to get the number of webs and spaces that will fit onto the seat rail, as was shown in fig. 28A (page 77). If you have an odd number you will either have more spaces than webs or vice versa.

With a pencil, mark on the top of the front seat rail where the webbing will come. On dining room type chairs the Pirelli webbing is put on top of the seat rail.

Measure likewise and mark the back seat rail. If the back rail is shorter than the front rail, the webs will be slightly closer together on the back rail than on the front rail.

Measure likewise and mark on the top of each side rail.

Try to attach the new webbing at a place where there are no tack holes from the previous webbing tacks.

Starting at the back rail of your chair seat, take your roll of Pirelli webbing and place the end 13mm ($\frac{1}{2}$″) back

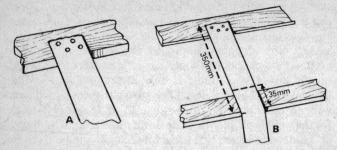

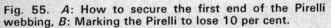

Fig. 55. *A*: How to secure the first end of the Pirelli webbing, *B*: Marking the Pirelli to lose 10 per cent.

in from the outside edge. Secure with four 16mm ($\frac{5}{8}$") improved tacks as shown in fig. 55A. It is not necessary to turn under the ends of Pirelli webbing as when using black and white webbing.

Lay the webbing across the chair frame to the front seat rail. With a biro or similar mark a line across the webbing level with the front edge of the seat rail.

Pirelli webbing needs to be stretched approximately 10% (i.e. by 10mm in every 100mm or 1" in every 10").

Measure the strand of Pirelli from the end behind the tacks to the biro line, subtract 10% and draw a second biro line (see fig. 55B).

You must now pull the Pirelli webbing forward until the second biro line is level with the front of the seat rail. At the same time as holding the stretched webbing forward attach it to the seat frame with four 16mm ($\frac{5}{8}$") improved tacks in the same formation as those at the other end of the webbing. This is one of those occasions when you could do with a third hand or a friend!

Cut the webbing 13mm ($\frac{1}{2}$") away from the tacks.

If you subtract less than 10% from the webbing, your seat will be rather soft and spongy, if more, rather harder, and on a small chair there is a risk of damaging the wood.

Make sure all tacks are driven in straight and fully. If the heads are not flush with the seat rail, they will cut into the webbing.

Complete all webbing in one direction first before starting to web in the other direction. When webbing your seat in the other direction, Pirelli webbing, like black and white webbing should be interlaced as when weaving. This was shown in fig. 29B, page 78.

FOAM

It is not necessary to put any material between Pirelli webbing and the foam. It would get undue wear unless the material is pleated in both directions to allow for the elasticity of the Pirelli webbing. The elastic sides of Pirelli webbing do not cut into the foam in the same way as traditional webbing does. Therefore place the foam directly on top of the Pirelli webbing.

However if you have used black and white traditional webbing, and on a small chair it is quite acceptable to do so, then cover the webbing with a piece of calico or similar to prevent the webbing cutting into the foam. Turn up an edge all round the calico and attach with 12mm ($\frac{1}{2}''$) tacks to the seat rail.

If you made a paper template of your seat and had the foam cut to the size and shape of your seat, you are now ready to start.

If however you bought a block of foam, you must now cut out the shape of your chair seat. Either draw a line round a paper template on the foam using a thick biro or, for a better seat edge, make two templates from hardboard or thick cardboard of your chair seat.

All templates must be 6mm ($\frac{1}{4}''$) larger all round than the outside rails of your chair seat.

If using hardboard make two holes in each of the templates, approximately 50mm (2") apart near the centre of the template, or further apart on larger seats. Place these two templates directly on top of one another with the block of foam in between.

Thread a needle with a double length of twine or strong string and push the needle down through one of the holes in the top template, through the foam and emerge through the hole in the second template directly under the first hole. This is shown in fig. 56A. Bring the needle and twine back up through the second set of holes. Secure the twine or string securely.

Using a serrated bread knife, and the two templates as a guide, cut the foam to the same size and shape as the two templates (see fig. 56B).

Cut the second piece of foam, this time from the 25mm (1″) thick piece. This should be 50mm (2″) smaller than the first piece. Spread some adhesive round the four sides of the top of the second piece of foam and place this centrally under the large piece of foam. Leave to dry.

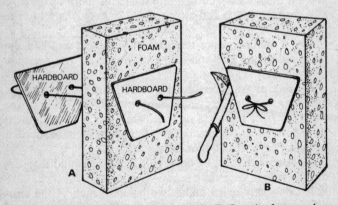

Fig. 56.   *A*: Threading the templates, *B*: Cut the foam using the templates as a guide.

CALICO STRIPS

Tear, rather than cut, four strips of calico, one for each side, back and front of the seat. The strips should be approximately 100mm (4″) deep by the length of the seat rail measured between the legs. Put a line of adhesive along one long edge of a calico strip and stick to the appropriate side. Do not stick the calico right up to the corners, it should only be attached to the foam opposite the space between the chair legs (see fig. 57A).

Leave overnight to dry. Dust with talcum powder to prevent the adhesive sticking to any outer covering if at all tacky.

Place the foam squarely and centrally on top of the Pirelli webbing and temporarily tack the strips of calico to the outsides of the seat frame with 13mm (½″) tacks, 40mm (1½″) apart. Pull the calico down fairly tightly.

Drive home all tacks when you are satisfied that the foam is correctly in position.

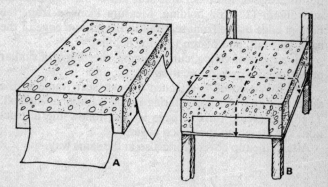

Fig. 57. A: Sticking the calico to the foam, B: Measuring for the terylene wadding.

TERYLENE WADDING

Measure from the bottom edge of the outside seat rail, up and over the foam and down to the bottom of the outside seat rail at the widest point (see fig. 57B).

Measure likewise from the bottom edge of the outside of the back seat rail, up and over the foam and down to the bottom of the front of the seat rail.

Cut a piece of Terylene wadding to size. Cut out corners as in fig. 40B, page 94. Lay this over the foam. It will be held in place by the calico cover.

CALICO COVER

The reason for having calico under the top cover and over the wadding and foam is threefold; first by having calico underneath, the life of the top cover is greatly increased, secondly it helps to keep out the strong sunlight which can deteriorate foam and thirdly it makes a good trial run before putting on your top cover. Unlike for a traditionally upholstered chair therefore, a calico cover is essential.

Measure from the bottom edge of one seat rail to the bottom edge of the other side seat rail at the widest point, add 50mm (2″) for holding. Measure likewise from the bottom edge of the front seat rail to the bottom edge of the back seat rail, add 50mm (2″) for holding.

Cut a piece of calico, curtain lining, sheeting or a similar new strongly woven fabric to size.

The calico cover is attached to your seat frame in the same way as when upholstering in the traditional method. Therefore please turn to page 95 and follow the instructions for attaching the calico cover.

Attach the top cover fabric also in the same way.

7

WING-BACKED CHAIR
THE TOP COVER

SHOPPING LIST

. . . m/yds top cover fabric   13mm tacks
. . . m/yds wadding   6 nails 25mm (1″) long
. . . m/yds piping cord   adhesive
   (*if appropriate*)   Black cloth – optional

To work out how much top cover fabric you need to buy for your chair and/or cushion, arm yourself with:
2 sheets of plain paper, approximately A4 size, i.e. 210mm x 300mm
Tape measure
Pencil or biro
Divide one sheet of paper into three columns. In the first column write the names of the various chair sections. Write "length" at the top of the second column and "width" at the top of the third column.

For example:

	LENGTH		WIDTH	
Inside back	90+15+5	=110cm	60+15+15+5	=95cm
Outside back	80+5	=85cm	70+5	=75cm
Seat	56+15+5	=76cm	50+15+15+5	=85cm
Inside Arm (2)	60+15+5	=80cm	68+15+5	=88cm
Outside Arm (2)	40+5	=45cm	90+5	=95cm
Inside Wing (2)	53+5	=58cm	50+15+5	=70cm
Outside Wing (2)	40+5	=45cm	30+5	=35cm
Front border	30+5	=35cm	56+5	=61cm
Arm front (2)	50+5	=55cm	20+5	=25cm
Cushion (if appropriate)				
Piping (if appropriate)				

Measure each section of the chair at the widest part that can be seen, add on to each measurement 50mm (2") for seam allowance and 150mm (6") for tuck-ins (i.e. that part which is hidden from view). Be generous with your measurements.

Take your second piece of paper and assume that the fabric is 122cm (48") wide unless you know differently. Mark out in squares/oblongs the various sections of the chair, marking in their names and measurements as shown in fig. 58.

It is a good idea before actually transferring the measurements of your chair to the second piece of paper to have an idea of the top cover fabric you wish to use. Some upholstery fabrics are wider than 122cm (48") and with the extra width two sections of the chair can be cut out side by side. Also note where the pattern comes in the fabric. For instance, is a bunch of flowers in the centre of the fabric or in the centre of each half? If this is the case you will not be able to lay out your chair sections as economically as the example here and each section will have to be centred on the fabric. Both these points will have a bearing on the amount of fabric needed.

The grain and any pattern must run in a straight line

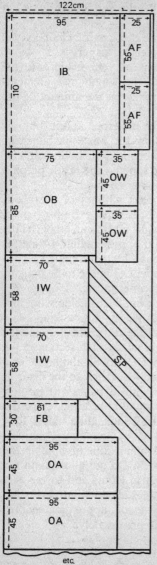

Key:
I.B. Inside back
O.B. Outside back
I.W. Inside wing
O.W. Outside wing
A.F. Arm front
F.B. Front border
O.A. Outside arm
S.P. Strips of piping

Measurements given are in centimetres.

Fig. 58. How to assess the amount of fabric needed. This type of layout continues, with the seat, the inside arm, the cushion, the cushion band, etc.

from the bottom to the top of the fabric cut for each section.

Tick off on your first list the sections of chair as you transfer them onto the second piece of paper.

Having transferred all sections of your chair onto the second piece of paper, add up the length measurements down the side of the paper to give you the amount of top cover fabric to buy.

However if using a distinctly patterned fabric buy an extra half metre or yard to allow for waste – a bunch of flowers must come in the centre of the chair back, seat, etc; the stalks disappearing over the top and the heads peeping up from the bottom wouldn't look at all good!

If you wish to pipe the various outlines of the chair, unless there is enough surplus fabric, allow extra for piping; e.g.; 1 metre of 122cm (48″) wide fabric cut 40mm (1½″) wide (on the cross) will give you approximately 14 metres of piping, which should be enough for your chair.

If you wish to save on the amount of fabric to be bought, add "flies", i.e.; tuck-ins of a cheaper fabric.

The patterns on each inside arm, each inside wing and each arm front should match as nearly as possible.

A golden rule – before cutting a particular section "measure twice and cut once"! Cut out each section in the form of a square/oblong. Do not try to cut the fabric into shape, this is done while attaching the fabric to the chair.

Mark each section as it is cut with its name written on a piece of paper and attached with cotton or a pin. Once the pieces have been cut they will all look alike unless they have been marked.

WADDING: Measure the length and width of both inside wings, inside arms and inside back. Do not allow extra for turnings. Measure likewise the arm fronts and to the arm fronts only add 25mm (1″) turnings all the way round.

Terylene wadding comes in a roll approximately 27″ wide and cotton wadding 23″ approximately.

Wing-backed chairs come in many sizes and are upholstered in a great variety of methods, some will be upholstered traditionally, and may or may not have a loose cushion on the seat, others may or may not have a loose cushion on a seat upholstered with foam and others have a loose cushion sitting straight onto a base of springs. Therefore this chapter is designed to be used for the recovering of any chair/sofa with arms and/or wings.

Whatever your chair, start by removing the loose cushion, if your chair has one. Turn your chair upside down, remove the black cloth or similar if any, and remove from the bottom rail all the tacks holding the present top cover. If you are going to reupholster the seat completely then remove all tacks from the bottom rail.

The outside back fabric will be stitched down each side, cut this stitching all the way up both sides, throw the fabric over to the front of the chair and remove the tacks holding the fabric to the top of the chair back. Note how this "back-tacking" using strips of cardboard is done. You will be using this method later.

Remove the fabric from the arm front. If there is cardboard or a wooden facing inside, preserve them carefully. This facing may need easing away from the arm fronts if it has been nailed in place.

Remove the fabric from the outside of both arms in a similar way to the back. Remove the fabric from the outside of both wings also.

Remove as many as necessary of the tacks holding the fabric at the base of the chair back and arms to allow the old seat cover to be completely removed.

If you need to reupholster the seat of your chair, apart from the seat do not strip the old top cover fabric from the inside sections of the chair until the new seat has been built up. The fabric will protect the upholstery until you are ready to attach the new top cover fabric.

It may be that your chair seat has serpentine or zig-zag springs, with only a loose cushion on the top. Check that these springs are still sound and discard if they are slack. Replace with new springs of a similar construction or the seat can be webbed using Pirelli webbing (see page 121 and follow the instructions).

Remove the existing top cover fabric which is covering the edges of the seat and replace in the same way with new top cover fabric with new wadding between the seat rails and the fabric if necessary. Back-tack the fabric to the seat front. To back-tack, see page 138 for back-tacking the fabric to the inside arms.

It is worth attaching a piece of black cloth, hessian or calico over the top of the springs or Pirelli webbing to lengthen the life of your loose cushion cover.

Measure across the seat from from side to side and add on 125mm (5") to allow for a 25mm (1") turn under on each side and a 75mm (3") pleat in the centre of the seat. This pleat will "give" when the seat is sat on.

Measure likewise from front to back of the seat and add on 125mm (5") for a pleat and turn unders.

If your chair seat has been upholstered in the traditional way and you wish to reupholster it as it was before, remaking the seat with springs and fibre, please turn to page 103 and follow directions for a sprung seat. If there are no springs in the chair, then follow directions for an unsprung seat, see page 73.

If you have never upholstered before perhaps you would rather start your upholstery in a slightly easier way by using foam. In that case, or *if your chair seat is already upholstered with foam* which needs replacing, please turn to page 119 and follow directions for an upholstered seat using foam.

If your traditional or foam seat is still in good repair, remove only the tacks holding the old top cover fabric.

With the work on your seat now completed carefully remove the old top cover fabric from the inside of the arms, wings and back.

Check all padding on the arms, wings and back; secure

in place if the padding has dropped but is still in good order.

If you have serpentine or zig-zag springs across the back of your chair, check that these are still held firmly in place and that they have not damaged the hessian. If the hessian has become worn or torn, carefully remove the entire padding on the back, which may have been sewn into a calico "bag", tack on a new piece of hessian and refix the stuffing by stitching the two together using a needle and twine and making long tacking stitches in rows 150mm (6") apart.

If you haven't already done so, cut the various chair sections out of your top cover fabric in block form. Do not cut the sections into shape. It is not recommended that you use your old top cover fabric as a pattern; in practice you will be lucky if it fits. If you do, allow ample extra round all sides, at least 50mm (2").

A new layer of either Terylene or Cotton wadding over the old will help the life of the new fabric, will cover up and keep in dirty patches and will do wonders for the chair's final appearance. Lay the wadding over the top of the old wadding or foam; this will be held in place by the new top cover fabric.

Starting with the inside back, place the oblong piece of fabric centrally over the chair back, bending inwards the excess fabric on both sides (see fig. 59A).

With a hand on each side of one back upright strut, feel with your fingers for the wooden rails joining the top and bottom of the wings and the arm to the back. There will always be two rails on each side and occasionally three.

Cut inwards from the outside of the fabric towards the centre of the wooden rail, stopping 25mm (1") away from the rail. Make a small notch, i.e. a cut to the left and to the right towards the outsides of the rail stopping 13mm ($\frac{1}{2}$") away from the rail. The fabric will then lie neatly and flat either side of the rail. Cut the fabric likewise for each rail.

Fold the fabric through to the back and secure with a few

temporary tacks, pulling the fabric taut (see fig. 59B).

N.B. If you are using a proper upholstery fabric it is not necessary to fold the fabric, the tacks will hold the single fabric quite adequately. However if your fabric is thin or frays easily, it would be safer to place the tacks through a fold of the fabric.

Cut the fabric in the same way to bypass the two back upright struts at the bottom of the inside back. Fold the fabric upwards and again feeling with your fingers, cut down from the edge of the fabric opposite where the struts come, stopping 25mm (1″) away from the strut. Make a notch as for the sides.

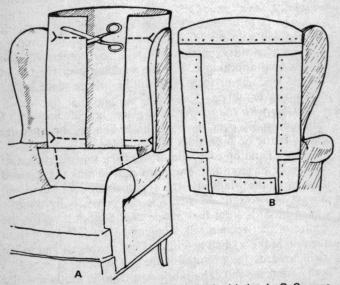

Fig. 59.   A: Placing the fabric for the inside back, B: Secure the fabric at the back.

Using 13mm ($\frac{1}{2}''$) tacks, temporarily tack the bottom of the fabric either to the back of the rail across the bottom of the chair back, or to the rail where the seat fabric was attached. Temporarily tack the top of the fabric, over the top of the chair back and attach to the back rail across the top of the chair back.

Having got the fabric centred and temporarily tacked, run the knuckle of your right hand from the centre of the chair back, upwards and at the same time pulling the fabric taut with your left hand. If necessary, and it most probably will be, adjust the tacks with your right hand. This is where a third hand or a friend is of help. Tighten the fabric and add tacks where necessary across the chair back at the top. Do likewise across the bottom of the back and finally both sides.

When you are satisfied that the top cover fabric has been pulled as tightly as possible and there are no wrinkles in the fabric, drive in all tacks fully and trim back the fabric to within 25mm ($1''$) of the tacks.

Next the inside wings. You may find it easier before attaching to pin the fabric into position with a few dress-making pins, stand back away from the chair and see that both inside wings match one another and that the weave runs correctly.

In the same way as for the back, feel with your fingers for the rails to be cut round. Snip the fabric so it lies smoothly where the top of the inside wing joins the inside back.

You will also have to snip the fabric where the wing joins the top of the arm, so that the fabric lays snugly on the arm (see fig. 60A). You will not be able to tack this bit, but in due course it will be sewn to the arm cover.

The fabric at the bottom of the inside wing will be temporarily tacked with 13mm ($\frac{1}{2}''$) tacks to the rail between the bottom of the wing and the inside arm. These tacks will be covered by the inside arm fabric.

The fabric at the side nearest the back will be taken

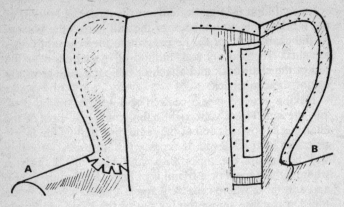

Fig. 60. *A*: Snip the fabric where the wing joins the top of the arm, *B*: Take fabric through and attach to outside of back upright strut.

through and attached to the outside of the back upright strut (see fig. 60B).

Drive in all temporary tacks and trim back the fabric to within 25mm (1″) of the tacks.

Work the other inside wing in the same way.

Next the inside arms. These are attached in the same way as for the back.

Lay the fabric over the top of the arm making sure there is sufficient fabric to go round to the front of the arm and also through to the back of the chair.

Again, sometimes it is helpful to pin both inside arms in position with dressmaking pins, stand back and look to see that both arms match, especially along the arm tops.

Using 13mm (½″) tacks, temporarily tack the outside edge of the fabric to the outside of the top rail of the arm front from the front edge back as far as where the arm joins the wing. Turn the fabric back and cut a line 50mm

(2″) away from the wing (see fig. 61A). Do not cut in too far, not quite to the inside edge of the front of the wing. Make a few snips in the fabric and turn under so that the fold meets the fabric covering the wing.

Turn up the fabric at the base of the arm, cut a notch opposite the upright strut at the front of the arm. Turn in

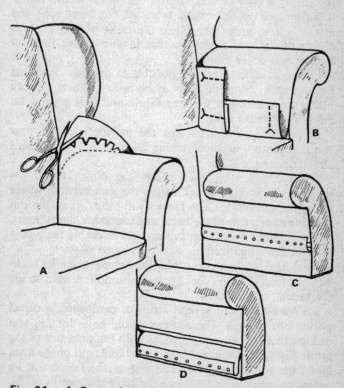

Fig. 61. *A*: Cut and notch the fabric to fit neatly round the wing, *B*: Cut notches opposite the struts, take inside arm fabric through to the outside of chair arm and either *C*: attach to bottom arm strut or *D*: seat rail

the fabric at the back and cut another notch along the bottom rail of the inside arm so that the resulting flap can be taken through to be tacked to the outside of the back (see fig. 61B).

Temporarily tack the bottom flap to the outside of the crossways rail at the bottom of the arm (fig. 61C). Alternatively attach the fabric to the bottom seat rail on the outside (fig. 61D). This will stop "things" being lost down inside. Turn up and cut off excess fabric at the front edge and attach rest to arm front. Keep the tacks well in towards centre of the arm fronts so that in due course the arm facings will cover the tacks.

Pull the fabric as taut as possible in the way described for the back, adjusting tacks as necessary. When you can make no wrinkles in the arm fabric and it is a good fit, drive in all tacks fully.

Piping. If you wish to pipe the outside edges of your chair, make up sufficient piping as described in the next chapter, see page 145.

Using 13mm ($\frac{1}{2}''$) tacks attach the piping round the outside edge of both wings, across the arm between where the inside and outside arm fabrics will meet, across the top and down each side of the back, and round both arm fronts. Snip the fabric on all bends or corners to enable the piping to lie flat (see fig. 62A).

The outside arms come next, and these must be back-tacked along the top edge, because you do not want to see the tacks.

To back-tack: Cut several strips of cardboard, a cereal packet box is ideal. These strips should be as long as you can cut them by 13mm ($\frac{1}{2}''$) wide. With the right side of the fabric facing the wooden rail across the length of the arm, cover the top 25mm (1"). The rest of the fabric will lie across the arm top and fall into the chair seat (see fig. 62B).

Place a strip of cardboard on the fabric, the long straight edge of the cardboard along the top edge of the cross rail. Temporarily tack with a few tacks. Check the position, making sure all tacks holding the inside arm fabric are hidden from view. If all is well and none show, add a few more tacks in between those already in. Tacks should be approximately 50mm (2″) apart. Drive all tacks in fully.

Let the top cover fabric fall down to the bottom of the outside of the arm and attach with tacks taking the fabric round and attaching to the back and arm fronts. Attach the fabric to the underside of the chair seat, cut the fabric by each leg, trim and fold under 13mm (½″) of fabric across the top of each leg (see (fig. 62C).

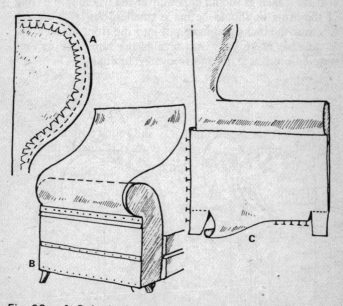

Fig. 62. *A*: Snip the fabric on all bends to enable the piping to lie flat, *B*: Back-tacking the outside arm along the top edge, *C*: Attaching fabric to underside of chair seat.

The outside back fabric must be "back-tacked" along the top of the chair back. Trim and fold under, down each side and secure with dress making pins. Attach the fabric to the underside of the chair seat, cutting the fabric by each leg, trim and turn under 13mm ($\frac{1}{2}$") of fabric above each chair leg.

The fold down each side of the outside back must be sewn with a matching thread. You may find this operation easier if you have a half circular needle. Instructions for ladder stitch used to join two pieces of fabric together, see page 100.

Now for the arm fronts. Make a template from or reuse the existing wooden or cardboard arm front facings. The arm front facings should either cover the whole of the front of the arms or should be made smaller, but large enough to cover the tacks you have put into the front of the arms. If possible make your arm facings the same size as they were before you started to recover your chair.

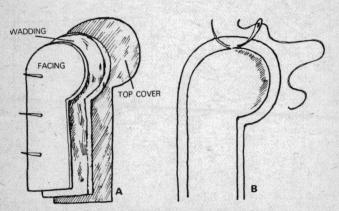

Fig. 63. *A*: Arm front in layers, *B*: Stitch arm fronts to chair.

If these facings are made from hardboard, drill three holes in the facing.

Cut two pieces of terylene wadding or similar 25mm (1″) larger all round than the arm facing, one for each arm. Cut two similar sized pieces from the top cover fabric, making sure the patterns for both arm fronts are similar.

Place three 25mm (1″) nails, one in each of the three holes, cover with wadding and the top cover fabric, attaching the edges to the back of the facing with adhesive (see fig. 63A). Using a bradawl make holes in the arm fronts opposite where the nails will come and gently drive the nails in the arm front facings into the holes started with the bradawl. Cover the head of your hammer with a double thickness of top cover fabric and be careful not to mark the fabric of the arm fronts.

Stitch carefully round the edges, again using a half circular needle for ease (see fig. 63B). The line of stitches can be covered with a matching cord to hide all stitches. This cord should be carefully sewn on hiding the stitches under the cord.

The underside of the seat can now be covered with a piece of black cloth or similar, cut 25mm (1″) larger all round than the bottom of the chair seat. Turn under the 25mm (1″) edge and tack with 13mm (½″) tacks to the underside of the chair seat.

8

FITTED CUSHION COVER

SHOPPING LIST

... m/yds Calico (if
    covering foam)
... m/yds top cover fabric
... "zip"
Tape measure
... m/yds Piping cord

Pins
Sewing cotton
Scissors
Chalk
Sewing machine

Most of the above ingredients on the shopping list you will have already, so it is just to remind you to gather them all up.

CALICO: If you have bought a new piece of foam for the interior of your cushion, you will need to cover it with calico before making up the top cover fabric. The measurements will be the same as for the top cover, except that of course you do not need to pipe the calico or put a zip in.

ZIP: Decide what length of zip is required. A zip generally will run across the centre of the back border stopping 50mm (2″) or so from each corner. Alternatively if you have a cushion made from a block of foam which will be in a chair with solid arms, then for ease of inserting the foam, take the zip round the corners and 25mm (1″) or so down each side.

Zips can be bought in lengths of multiples of 50mm (2″), i.e.; 350mm (14″), 400mm (16″), 450mm (18″) etc.

TOP COVER FABRIC: Measure the length of the cushion from the back to the front excluding the border. To this measurement add 50mm (2″) for seam allowance. Measure likewise across the cushion at the widest point for the width measurement and add 50mm (2″) for seam allowance.

If you are lucky you may well be able to get the cushion top and cushion bottom out side by side from one 122cm (48″) wide piece of top cover fabric.

FOR THE BORDER: If you have a distinctive pattern, the length measurement must be from the bottom to the top of the border. However if you are working with a plain fabric the length measurement can either be top to bottom of the border or round the border of the cushion. This can be very helpful when one has a long narrow piece of fabric left over from upholstering the chair which often runs down the selvedge edge of the fabric.

Measure round the entire border of your cushion and subtract the length of your zip and add 50mm (2″). Measure likewise the depth of your cushion border and add 50mm (2″).

You will also need two strips of top cover fabric to go either side of your zip. Each width measurement needs to be the length of the zip plus 75mm (3″). Each length measurement will be half the width of the border plus 50mm (2″), i.e.; 25mm (1″) for turnunder by the zip and 25mm (1″) for seam allowance.

If you are piping your cushion, and it certainly adds to both looks and length of life, allow extra fabric. Remember the piping should be cut on the cross.

PIPING CORD: Piping cord can be bought in various sizes, No. 3 being the most usual for cushion covers unless your fabric is very heavy then No. 4 would be preferable. It is worth washing your cord before making it up as cotton cords tend to shrink when wet.

SEWING COTTON: Buy cotton if your top cover fabric is made from a natural fibre, such as cotton or linen, or polyester cotton if your fabric is made from a man-made fibre.

Having bought your fabric, gather up a good pair of sharp scissors, a long ruler, a tape measure and a piece of blackboard or tailor's chalk.

The first job will be to make a fitted calico cover for your foam cushion if it doesn't already have one. This will considerably lengthen the life of the foam and ensure that the top cover fabric will look and wear better.

The calico cover is made up in exactly the same way as the top cover fabric except of course you do not need to pipe the seams nor put in a zip. The border can be made as one long continuous strip. Machine all seams except one edge through which the foam cushion can be inserted. Finish off by hand.

If your cushion is feather- or down-filled and is beginning to leak, you should do the same thing, but instead of using calico you must use a down-proof cambric. Put the feathers still in the old bag straight into the new bag; otherwise the new bag must have two walls built across the cushion to keep the feathers in their three separate compartments.

CUTTING: Measure your cushion accurately and cut out two square/oblong pieces 50mm (2″) larger all round than the actual cushion, one piece for the top and the other for the bottom part of your cushion. Make sure the pattern is centred and runs from the front towards the back. If your cushion is an odd shape, cut out a paper pattern first and try for size.

PIPING: Piping fabric is generally cut on the cross, thus enabling it to stretch round corners, and the end result looks better.

Piping strips can either be made out of odd pieces of fabric left over from the upholstery of your chair or a quarter of a metre/yard width of fabric.

To get the true cross, make sure all four edges of your piece of fabric are cut along the warp and weft, take a corner of your fabric and turn up so that the two measurements of the piece turned back measure the same (see fig. 64A). Cut across the diagonal.

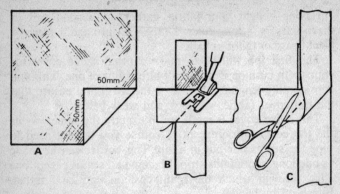

Fig. 64. *A*: To get the true cross, turn up a corner and cut across the diagonal, *B*: To join, lay one strip across the other at right angles and machine, *C*: Trim and press.

For a No. 3 piping cord, cut strips 40mm (1½″) wide. Join the strips together by laying one strip on top of another at a 90° angle. Machine across at a 45° angle (see fig. 64B). Trim and press (see fig. 64C). Insert piping cord into the strip and machine using an ordinary sewing foot.

With a piece of chalk and a long ruler if you have got one, mark out where the seam lines should come onto each of the two pieces of top cover fabric. Take a length of made up piping and, starting in the centre of the back, lay the piping along the chalk line, pin as far as the corner. Exactly where the piping meets the chalk line at the corner, cut into the fabric covering the piping right up to the cord itself (see fig. 65A). This will ensure that the piping will lie nicely round the corner. Repeat at each corner.

Carry on pinning until you get back to where you started, then overlap the two ends by 50mm (2″) and cut the piping. The fabric round the cord must now be joined and the seam must be on the cross. Undo the first pin, open up the piping

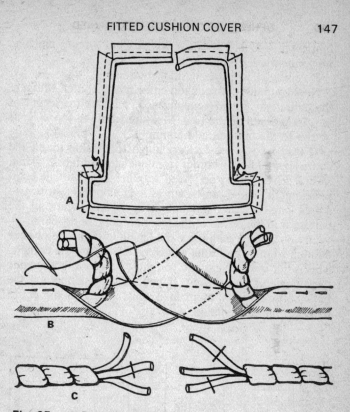

Fig. 65.   *A*: Position of piping on cushion cover, *B*: Joining the piping, *C*: Splicing the cord.

at both ends so the fabric will lie flat and lay one end on top of the other end at right angles (see fig. 65B). Pin and machine across at 45° angle.

The two pieces of cord must now be spliced (see fig. 65C). Cut two of the three ends on one side and one of the three ends away on the other side. Wind the three protruding cords together, bind with sewing cotton and cover with the fabric strip. Using your zipper or piping foot, machine round the whole cushion top.

Do likewise with the cushion bottom.

Now you must cut your top cover fabric border. Measure the entire way round your cushion, subtract the length of the zip and add 50mm (2"). Measure from the top of your border to the bottom, add 50mm (2").

It may be you are lucky enough to be able to get the entire length of your border from one piece of fabric; if not, several lengths must be joined together to make one complete length. These can be cut as long as possible with two seams, one on either side but make sure the centre of the pattern is in the centre of the front border (see fig. 66A).

Or you can cut each piece the length of each side of your cushion so that the seams will come exactly on the corners. This is not quite so easy as you must be very exact in your measurements and sewing. If you do use this method the back section with the zip in it must be made the entire length of the back section.

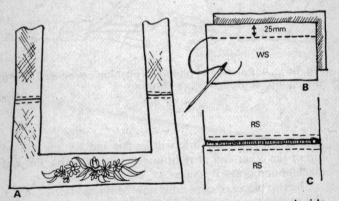

Fig. 66. *A*: Border cut with two seams, one on each side, *B*: The back section: tack the two right sides together, *C*: Pin or tack the zip in position.

For the back section, cut two lengths of fabric, each length being the length of your zip plus 75mm (3″) by half the depth of the border plus 50mm (2″). The zip will go horizontally across the centre of the back section so that your cushion will be completely reversible and the zip will not show whichever way up your cushion is.

Take the two sections just cut that will go either side of your zip, lay them together with the right sides facing and tack the two together 25mm (1″) in along one long edge (see fig. 66B). (It is necessary to tack this with cotton, do not pin on this occasion).

Press the seam open and lay over the zip (see fig. 66C). Pin or tack the zip in position. Using the piping or zipper foot of your machine, machine stitch close to either side of the zip. Take out your tacking thread. This back section of the border should now be the same width as the rest of the border section.

Tack or pin the border fabric to the fabric with the zip in it at one end and machine stitch (see fig. 67A). Leave the

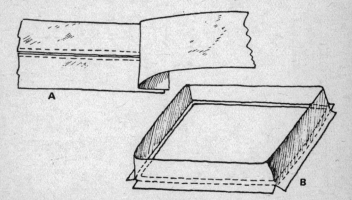

Fig. 67. *A*: Tack the zip section to the rest of the border fabric, *B*: Machine stitch round the border, cutting into the fabric at each corner.

other end unpinned and unsewn for the moment. The whole border is now in one long piece.

Allowing 25mm (1") seam allowance pin the border to one of the cushion sections. Start at the back and pin round. Where the two ends of the border section meet, pin and machine. Machine stitch round the entire border, cutting into the border fabric at each corner to enable the fabric to lie smoothly at the corner (see fig. 67B).

Undo and make sure the zip is open, otherwise when the border is machined round both top and bottom of your cushion, you won't be able to turn the cushion right side outwards!

Pin border round the second of the cushion sections and machine stitch. Press all seams.

If you have a zig-zag stitch on your machine, trim and neaten all seams.

INDEX

PAPERFRONTS FOR THE FAMILY

CHILDREN'S PARTY AND GAMES BOOK

Over 100 games to suit children of all ages. Includes helpful ideas for invitations, food, and ten *themes* for special parties.

BABIES NAMES A-Z

Choose your baby's name! Your child's name is important — it has got to last for life! 3,000 names and their meanings are given to help you find the right one.

HOME MEDICAL ENCYCLOPEDIA

All illnesses and medical terms appear in A-Z order for easy reference. No medical terms unfamiliar to the layman are used.

EASYMADE WINE & COUNTRY DRINKS

Make your own wine for as little as a few pence per bottle! No expensive equipment is required and many of the ingredients can be found in field and hedgerow.

WEDDING ETIQUETTE PROPERLY EXPLAINED

Covers all the major aspects such as legal requirements, the banns, the Church service under all denominations and planning your reception.

All uniform with this book

ELLIOT RIGHT WAY BOOKS, KINGSWOOD BUILDINGS, LOWER KINGSWOOD, TADWORTH, SURREY, U.K.

PAPERFRONTS FOR THE PET OWNER

RIGHT WAY TO KEEP DOGS

All you need to know about dogs — breeds, training, shows and diseases are covered. Officially recommended by the National Canine Defence League.

RIGHT WAY TO KEEP CATS

Complete guide to keeping your cat in the best of health, whatever its breed or variety.

HORSEKEEPERS ENCYCLOPEDIA

A practical up-to-date guide for all horse keepers. It emphasises the need to ensure the comfort and well-being of the animal, since a well-kept horse is a healthy one.

RIGHT WAY TO RIDE A HORSE

Simple instructions and explanations, plus authoritative attention to details mark this book among the great.

RIGHT WAY TO KEEP PONIES

Whether you are thinking of getting your first pony, or have one already this book is planned to improve your knowledge and provide the information necessary to keep the animal in tip-top health.

All uniform with this book
**ELLIOT RIGHT WAY BOOKS,
KINGSWOOD BUILDINGS,
LOWER KINGSWOOD, TADWORTH,
SURREY, U.K.**

OUR PUBLISHING POLICY

HOW WE CHOOSE

Our policy is to consider every deserving manuscript and we can give special editorial help where an author is an authority on his subject but an inexperienced writer. We are rigorously selective in the choice of books we publish. We set the highest standards of editorial quality and accuracy. This means that a *Paperfront* is easy to understand and delightful to read. Where illustrations are necessary to convey points of detail, these are drawn up by a subject specialist artist from our panel.

HOW WE KEEP PRICES LOW

We aim for the big seller. This enables us to order enormous print runs and achieve the lowest price for you. Unfortunately, this means that you will not find in the *Paperfront* list any titles on obscure subjects of minority interest only. These could not be printed in large enough quantities to be sold for the low price at which we offer this series. We sell almost all our *Paperfronts* at the same unit price. This saves a lot of fiddling about in our clerical departments and helps us to give you world-beating value. Under this system, the longer titles are offered at a price which we believe to be unmatched by any publisher in the world.

OUR DISTRIBUTION SYSTEM

Because of the competitive price, and the rapid turnover, *Paperfronts* are possibly the most profitable line a bookseller can handle. They are stocked by the best bookshops all over the world. It may be that your bookseller has run out of stock of a particular title. If so, he can order more from us at any time—we have a fine reputation for "same day" despatch, and we supply any order, however small (even a single copy), to any bookseller who has an account with us. We prefer you to buy from your bookseller, as this reminds him of the strong underlying public demand for *Paperfronts*. Members of the public who live in remote places, or who are housebound, or whose local bookseller is unco-operative, can order direct from us by post.

FREE

If you would like an up-to-date list of all paperfront titles currently available, send a stamped self-addressed envelope to
ELLIOT RIGHT WAY BOOKS, BRIGHTON RD.,
LOWER KINGSWOOD, SURREY, U.K.